ATTRACTIVE

COMMUNICATION

300 WAYS
TO MAKE COMMUNICATION
MORE ATTRACTIVE

MICHAEL ROONI, JURIS DOCTOR

ATTRACTIVE COMMUNICATION
HARDCOVER EDITION USA $29.95
ISBN: 978-0-9857821-7-7
WWW.ATTRACTIVECOMMUNICATION.COM

ATTRACTIVE COMMUNICATION
TABLE OF CONTENTS

INTRODUCTION 1

PART 1: INTERPERSONAL COMMUNICATION 3

Chapter 1	Attractive Greetings and Goodbyes	5
Chapter 2	Personal Software	11
Chapter 3	Respect	15
Chapter 4	Integrity	21
Chapter 5	Interpersonal Gratitude	25
Chapter 6	Communicative Gifting	29
Chapter 7	Compliments	33
Chapter 8	Congratulations and Special-Day Greetings	37
Chapter 9	Smiles and Humor	41
Chapter 10	Excitement	45
Chapter 11	Confidence without Arrogance	49
Chapter 12	Beneficial Ambition without Greed or Envy	51
Chapter 13	Communication Type Congruence	55
Chapter 14	Verbal, Non-Verbal, and Mode Matching	61
Chapter 15	Attractive Questioning	65
Chapter 16	Attractive Feedback	71
Chapter 17	Responsive Response	77
Chapter 18	Apologies and Forgiveness	81
Chapter 19	Best Wishes and Encouragement	85
Chapter 20	Intact Communication Bridges	89

PART 2: NON-VERBAL COMMUNICATION 93

Chapter 21	Attractive Non-Verbal Communication	95
Chapter 22	Visual Image	101

PART 3: COMMUNICATION TIMING AND
SURROUNDINGS 103

Chapter 23	Appointments	105
Chapter 24	Surroundings	109
Chapter 25	Punctuality	113
Chapter 26	Good Moods	117
Chapter 27	Patience	121
Chapter 28	Brevity	125

PART 4: LISTENING 129

Chapter 29 Participatory Listening 131
Chapter 30 Listening Manifestations 135
Chapter 31 Attracted Listening 137
Chapter 32 Speaker-Focused Listening 141
Chapter 33 No-Solution Listening 145
Chapter 34 No Multitasking 149

PART 5: PERSUASION AND DISPUTE RESOLUTION 153

Chapter 35 Credibility 155
Chapter 36 Limited Availability of Offerings 159
Chapter 37 Value Communication 161
Chapter 38 Comparisons and Confirmations 165
Chapter 39 Examples, Anecdotes, and Quotes 169
Chapter 40 Flexibility 173
Chapter 41 Complaint Modification 175
Chapter 42 Attractive Response 181
Chapter 43 Repetition 183
Chapter 44 Commonality 187
Chapter 45 Mutual Fairness 191
Chapter 46 Reasonable Conclusions 195
Chapter 47 Switching Shoes 197
Chapter 48 Image Facilitation 201
Chapter 49 Supplemental Facilitation 207
Chapter 50 Declining Communication 211
Chapter 51 Promise Requesting 217
Chapter 52 Interim Solutions 221
Chapter 53 Mediation 225
Chapter 54 Mediation Variations 231

PART 6: INTRAPERSONAL COMMUNICATION 235

Chapter 55 Inner Gratitude Messaging 237
Chapter 56 Attractive Imagination 243
Chapter 57 Inner Declarations 247
Chapter 58 Inner Optimism Messaging 251
Chapter 59 Inner Resilience Messaging 253
Chapter 60 Inner Fear Messaging 257
Chapter 61 Inner Keys 261
Chapter 62 Inner Stress Reduction 265

CONCLUSION 269

ABOUT THE AUTHOR 271

ATTRACTIVE COMMUNICATION
INTRODUCTION

Communication impacts all of us in this world in very powerful ways, each and every day. We communicate in our personal lives. We communicate in our business lives. We communicate when we have to resolve issues or disputes. We communicate with ourselves through "self-talk" every time we have a thought. We communicate with our eyes, facial expressions, body expressions, postures, gestures, and mannerisms. Even the tones of our voices, the distances we keep, and the ways we touch others constitute communication.

When we think of "attractive" things that we would like to have, we usually think in terms of attractive bodies, faces, homes, offices, cars, paintings, jewelry, furniture, computers, electronics, clothes, etc. However, I invite each and every person in this world to also consider having the most attractive communication possible. Attractive communications attract great personal relationships. Attractive communications attract rewarding business relationships. Attractive communications attract friendly and cooperative resolutions of disputes. Attractive "self-talk" communications attract inner peace, resilience, confidence, enthusiasm, and happiness. The effects of attractive communication are powerful, meaningful, and lasting. I believe with all of my heart, mind, and soul that one of the fastest and most powerful ways to elevate the attractiveness of our lives is to elevate the attractiveness of our communications. I wrote this book in order to help make that happen.

Because I know that your time is valuable, I have written this book with short and to-the-point chapters. Each of these 62 chapters includes not only one element of *Attractive Communication* but also an Action Plan to implement it. Each Action Plan sets forth practical ways you can elevate the attractiveness of your communication.

I invite you to regard this book as an attractive communication toolbox with 300 ways or tools you can use right away. Of the 300 ways or tools, 100 relate to Interpersonal Communication or communication between people; 12 relate to Non-Verbal Communication or communication without words; 32 relate to Communication Timing and Surroundings; 32 relate to Listening; 87 relate to Persuasion and Dispute Resolution; and last but not least, 37 relate to Intrapersonal Communication or "self-talk."

As you read *Attractive Communication*, think about how you can apply the concepts to your own communications and life circumstances. Join me in this life-changing journey toward attaining the most attractive, effective, and savvy communication.

PART I:

INTERPERSONAL COMMUNICATION

Attractive Communication
Chapter 1
Attractive Greetings and Goodbyes

Before jumping into the content of our communications with those we are communicating with, we can increase the attractiveness of our communications by expressing attractive greetings. After communicating the content of our communications, we can elevate the attractiveness of our communications by expressing attractive goodbyes.

If our greetings are attractive, we make a great communicative first impression. If our goodbyes are attractive, we will leave a great communicative last impression. How we greet people sets the tone and mood for communicating in the moment. Our goodbyes do the same for communicating in the future.

Our greetings should be polite, warm, caring, and positive, delivered with proper etiquette. Attractive in-person greetings—both business and personal—include eye contact, a smile, a handshake if appropriate, and an acknowledgment that we are happy to see them. In personal interactions, we can add a hug, a "high-five," or a pat on the back. Caring greetings entail at least one or two questions about how the person is doing, what is new, and other friendly questions. Positive greetings convey that we bring a positive attitude to our time together and our anticipated communication.

The most attractive goodbyes are also polite, warm, caring, and positive, delivered with proper etiquette.

ACTION PLAN
FOR ATTRACTIVE GREETINGS AND GOODBYES

WAY 1
Business takes place between real people, and so do personal interactions. Don't forget to be personable!

Manifest warmth by maintaining eye contact and genuinely smiling as much as possible and practical under the circumstances. # WAY 2

WAY 3
Conduct yourself in a caring manner. Caring greetings—whether in a business or personal setting—involve at least one or two questions about how the person you are communicating with is doing, what is new, and so on. Similarly, caring goodbyes include a warm statement of best wishes.

Conduct yourself with a positive energy. Positive greetings, whether in a business or personal setting, **WAY 4** should communicate your positive attitude toward your meeting and the subject matter of your communication. You can say something like this:

"I'm very happy to be meeting with you today."

"It's wonderful to see you."

"I'm happy to be talking about _____ with you here and now."

Positive goodbyes—whether in a business or personal setting—entail communicating gratitude, enthusiasm, and optimism about future interactions.

In personal settings, you can say something like this:

"Thanks for getting together with me. I enjoyed seeing you and am excited to see you again soon. I'm sure we'll have a great time again."

In business settings, you can say something like this:

"Thank you for a great meeting. I look forward to working with you. I believe we will be successful."

WAY 5 In personal settings, acknowledge and attractively greet not only the person you are communicating with, but also his or her friends and family members who are present. If you do so, the friends and family members will typically comment on how polite and warm you were to them. Conversely, if you were cold and dismissive, they will typically comment on that as well.

In business settings, acknowledge and attractively **WAY 6** greet all staff you see, including personal assistants, clerks, drivers, secretaries, and so on. Give staff members the same respect and acknowledgment that you would give to managers and executives. If you "look down" on staff, their boss will hear about it and look down on you. Conversely, if you treat staff exceptionally well, they will tell their boss how polite and gracious you are.

WAY 7 When greeting others, don't "rush" to get to business. During the meeting, do not keep looking at your watch. When people feel rushed, they often think you don't care about them or that you lack manners.

In saying hello or goodbye, pay attention to what **WAY 8** the person you are communicating with prefers. For example, if the person being greeted seems quite formal, address him or her formally. You would say, "Hello, Mr. Smith." If the person seems to be more casual, you would say, "Hello, John." When in doubt, directly ask for greeting preferences by saying, "Is it okay if I call you John?" A more subtle approach is to observe the way you are spoken to and do the same in return as appropriate. For example, if you are called by your first name, then respond with a first name. If you are called by your last name, then respond with a last name.

WAY 9

In saying hello or goodbye, pay attention to cultural and regional customs as they pertain to what you say and do. If you know you'll be meeting someone from a different country than yours, research etiquette for that person's culture. Examples of cultural considerations include (but are not limited to) the following:

a. If you give a "thumbs up" when responding to a "hello, how are you?" when greeting people from certain parts of the Middle East, West Africa, and South America, you are actually making an offensive gesture.

b. If you give an "OK" sign when responding to a "hello, how are you?" from a person from Brazil, you are actually making a gesture similar to showing a "middle finger" in the U.S.

c. If you attempt to greet or say goodbye to a traditional woman from the Middle East by shaking her hand, giving her a hug, kissing her hand, or (worst of all) kissing her on the cheek, your greeting could be considered highly offensive.

d. When greeting a Japanese businessperson, if you are given a business card and you put your fingers on the text, fold the card without reviewing it, and/or put it in your back pocket, your greeting could be considered insulting.

e. If a person from Thailand gives you a "wai" greeting by placing his or her hands together and bowing, your failure to give a "wai" greeting in return may be considered rude, like refusing to shake his or her hand.

f. If you say hello to a Greek person by using a five-finger palm-out gesture without waving your hand adequately, you could be communicating what is called a "moutza" or "feces in your face" gesture. In Pakistan, showing the palm of the hand to another person can also be considered offensive.

g. After saying hello and sitting down, if you put your arm over the back of the chair of a person from Thailand, you would likely be insulting him or her.

h. After saying hello and sitting down, if you cross your legs with the bottom of your shoes visible to and/or pointed toward a person from the Middle East, he or she may be highly offended. Shoes are considered by many to be dirty in the Middle East.

Attractive Communication
Chapter 2
Personal Software

Just as computer software runs the operations of a computer, every one of us has customized *personal software* that runs our decisions in life. To communicate effectively with a real computer, we need to connect with its software through its hardware. Similarly, for us to communicate attractively and effectively with the people we communicate with, we need to connect with the "software" that runs their lives.

How can we determine a person's *personal software?* We accomplish that by analyzing and understanding that person's interests, experiences, feelings, preferences, ideals, and goals. People usually tell us about these if we simply ask them. They also leave important clues about what's important through their past communications and interactions—both with us and with others. Added to that are their websites, writings, blogs, resumes, networking postings, and other public expressions.

ACTION PLAN FOR PERSONAL SOFTWARE

To determine a person's *personal software*, start by asking about his or her interests, **WAY 10**

experiences, feelings, preferences, ideals, and goals. For example, you could ask these questions:

"What are a few of your interests?"

"What are some of your experiences with _____?"

"What are your feelings about _____?"

"How do you prefer to deal with _____?"

"What are your views on _____?"

"What are some things you'd like to achieve in your life?"

WAY 11 List everything you can remember about what the person you're communicating with has said to *you* in the past related to his or her interests, experiences, feelings, preferences, ideals, and goals.

List everything you can remember about what the person you're communicating with **WAY 12** has said to *others* in the past related to his or her interests, experiences, feelings, preferences, ideals, and goals.

WAY 13 Analyze websites, writings, blogs, resumes, networking postings, and other public expressions related to the interests, experiences, feelings, preferences, ideals, and goals of the person you're communicating with.

Focus on genuinely and positively connecting the content of your communications with the **WAY 14** interests, experiences, feelings, preferences, ideals, and goals of the person you're communicating with.

Attractive Communication
Chapter 3
Respect

Showing respect to others is powerfully and instantly attractive for several reasons. First, if we respect others, we promote openness in their communications with us. When they feel respected, they become engaged, open, and receptive to what we have to say. They have no need to get defensive; instead, they focus on understanding the content of our communications.

Second, if we respect others, people will see us in a positive light that will be favorably associated with the content of our communications. I call this *positive communicative association*. Conversely, if we disrespect others, people will see us in a negative light that will be unfavorably associated with what we communicate. I call this *negative communicative association*.

Third, respect—and lack thereof—is contagious. When we respect others, they often respect us in return. Similarly, if we disrespect others, they will likely disrespect us in return.

Respectful, attractive communications entail words that are self-expressive as opposed to combative or profane. Self-expressive statements start with "I," such as "I feel" or "I sense." Instead of pointing fingers and/or bringing others down, starting our sentences with "I" aims to express what we're experiencing without judging or demeaning others.

Respectful, attractive communications entail words in the form of a request as opposed to a command. Requests are polite and non-threatening. Conversely, commands reflect an image of superiority and domination. People at the receiving end of a command don't like to be debased, controlled, or ordered around. If we make commands and people respond to them, they can still resent us for it.

Respectful, attractive communications entail words in the form of a request as opposed to a complaint. A request is merely a polite call to action. Conversely, complaints often make others feel defensive, even insulted. Moreover, complaints negatively focus on problems while requests focus on solutions.

Respectful, attractive communications entail words that are *inviting* as opposed to *excluding*. Invitations for participation allow the people we communicate with to feel as though they matter and that they can make a difference. By making others feel part of our team when communicating with them, we show that we respect them and value their input. Conversely, by excluding others or "shutting them up," we can make them feel disrespected and taken for granted.

ACTION PLAN FOR RESPECT

WAY 15
Keep in mind that the more others like the way you treat them, the more favorably they will react to the content of your communications. Don't verbally attack people, even when you perceive them as being wrong or unfair. Instead, express how their actions are making you feel. Start your sentences with "I." For example, you can say the following:

"I feel _____."

"I sense that _____."

"I'm experiencing _____."

"I understand that _____."

Refrain from using accusatory words that start with "you." For example:

"You are a _____."

"You did _____."

"You caused_____."

Do not under any circumstance use profanity or personal insults. Even if someone insults

WAY 16
you, instead of escalating the situation, calm him or her down. Start your sentence with an "I." You might say something like the following:

"I feel that something is making you angry."

"I sense that you are not happy with _____."

"I understand that you are upset."

Follow up by asking questions like these:

"How can I cooperate with you to make things better?"

"Is there anything I can do to change the situation for the better?"

"I want to work with you so that you feel better. Tell me what you'd like me to do."

WAY 17
Do not command, order, direct, or mandate. Instead, make requests. Instead of saying "you must" or "you have to" or "do it because I said so," say something like this:

"I request that _____."

"I ask that we do _____."

"I would appreciate it if you would do _____ instead."

WAY 18
Do not repeatedly complain about problems. Instead, focus on solutions. You could say the following:

"Let's figure out how to _____."

"Would you like to proceed by doing _____?"

"It would make me happy if you _____."

"I request that you do _____ to address this situation."

WAY 19
As much as possible, invite others to participate in solving problems. Invite them

to share their thoughts with you. Communicate that you value their opinions and look forward to working with them to find solutions. You could say the following:

"I invite you to give me your opinion about how we can resolve
_____."

"Because I value your opinions, I invite you to work with me to
_____."

"What are your thoughts regarding _____ so we can move ahead?"

"I look forward to working with you as a team on _____."

Assume that, at all times, each word you **WAY 20** communicate is being recorded, videotaped, televised, broadcast, and downloaded to the Internet for everyone to see and hear. If you do so, you are likely to better monitor and filter the quality of the content of your communications. You will say things you can be proud of, not things you will later regret.

ATTRACTIVE COMMUNICATION
CHAPTER 4
INTEGRITY

Communication without integrity is one of the most unattractive communications of all. Even partial lack of integrity in communications is extremely unattractive. For example, I don't think many of us would be happy if our lovers are *kind of* faithful/loyal/honest in their relationships with us. Not many people would be happy if their lovers only *sometimes* cheated on them. Most bosses would not be happy if their employees only *sometimes* stole from them.

Dishonesty or lack of ethics indeed creates negative perceptions and destroys our communications. Communication that comes from a reliable, believable, and ethical source has a powerful, persuasive, and attractive presumption in its favor. Conversely, communication that comes from an unreliable, unbelievable, and unethical source has a tainted and unattractive presumption against it.

Integrity is a choice. We can choose to do the right thing. We can choose to adhere to an ethical standard. We can choose to have a good, clean energy. We can choose to treat others the way we would like to be treated. The choice of integrity is good for others. However, it is most beneficial for us. If we choose integrity, we will sleep better at night with a much lower risk of adverse consequences, we will be trusted and respected by others, and we will feel better about ourselves. People who are perceived as lacking in integrity do not get the benefit of the doubt from others. They will instead get heavy burdens of doubt from others. People without integrity carry the heavy burdens of doubt on their shoulders each and every day.

The intelligent, attractive choice of lifetime integrity in business and in personal interactions must be communicated to others with both our words and with our actions. We should incorporate into our personal lives and our businesses a specific discussion of the importance of integrity on a continual basis. For the right people, our communication of our own integrity—as well as our communication of the integrity we expect in return—is highly attractive. Typically, the people not attracted to the importance of integrity are the people we would probably not want to interact with.

ACTION PLAN FOR INTEGRITY

WAY 21 Communicate with integrity. If you communicate without integrity, the people

you communicate with won't trust you. Even when what you are saying is true at this moment, if you did not communicate with integrity in the past, you probably won't be believed!

Your integrity must be complete. Do not cut corners with integrity. Nobody likes or respects only partial integrity. # WAY 22

WAY 23
Incorporate discussions of the importance of integrity into your personal and business communications. For example, if you are on a date, you could say:

"I believe in complete honesty and loyalty in personal relationships; how do you feel about that?" If he or she looks away or exhibits non-verbal signs of discomfort with your question, you might have a problem. Consider following up by asking whether the person you are on a date with has cheated in a past relationship. If he or she says yes, you might have a problem.

As another example, if you are establishing a new business relationship, you can say: "I do business with complete honesty and integrity. I also believe in keeping my word. How do you feel about that?" If the response is enthusiastic and inviting, that is great. If you get no eye contact or a fake smile in return, you might have a problem.

Attractive Communication
Chapter 5
Interpersonal Gratitude

When we appreciate others, we transmit to them an attractive and positive energy. In turn, they become more receptive and attracted to us and what we have to say. Here are five important suggestions to follow.

First, as we think about or observe others, we should mindfully and continually seek qualities we appreciate about them and/or about their actions. We should have our "gratitude scanner" on at all times, finding as many things as possible to be thankful for.

Second, we should communicate our thankfulness with specificity. The more specific our expression of gratitude, the more effective it will be. This is because expressing gratitude with precise details communicates more consideration and acknowledgment than a general exchange of pleasantries.

Third, we should individualize our gratitude. For example, if we want to appreciate a group that has seven members, it's best to thank each member by name. Individual gratitude enriches our gratitude because most people love specific attention, specific acknowledgment, and the sound of their names. Conversely, group gratitude dilutes our gratitude because it makes it less personal.

Fourth, we should express our gratitude promptly. When our active search/scan for interpersonal gratitude yields a result, we should communicate our gratitude as soon as possible. Unlike fine wine, gratitude doesn't get better with age. In fact, I even suggest giving advance gratitude—that is, thanking others for things they have not yet done to encourage them in their efforts.

Fifth, we should tailor the expression of our gratitude to specific preferences. Some people may like receiving certificates, plaques, or public declarations. Others may simply prefer a smile or a handwritten note. Others may prefer receiving gifts or flowers. We should thank people in ways they *like* to be thanked. If we don't know what those ways are, we should find out.

ACTION PLAN FOR INTERPERSONAL GRATITUDE

Actively and continually seek reasons to thank people. Keep your "gratitude scanner" on at all times. **WAY 24**

WAY 25 Be specific with your expressions of gratitude. For example, you might say something like this:

"I appreciate your doing _____ because it _____."

"_____ has meant a lot to me because _____.
Thanks."

If possible, do not "group thank." Instead, identify each person by name individually. **WAY 26**
Again, people love the sound of their own names!

WAY 27 Anytime you have something to be thankful for, express your gratitude as soon as possible.
Do not let your feelings of gratitude "age."

Practice advance gratitude as much as possible. For example, if you are making a **WAY 28**
request, you might say something like this:

"Thank you in advance for your cooperation."

"Thank you ahead of time for your careful consideration."

"I appreciate your willingness to be open when dealing with the situation tomorrow."

WAY 29 People like to be thanked in different ways. Find out how they like to be appreciated and
then thank them in the way that is special to them. If you don't know, ask others for ideas or ask the person you want to thank directly. If

that's not practical, ask indirectly by posing a hypothetical situation. For example, you might ask something like this:

"If someone wanted to thank you for something, how would you like that person to show gratitude to you?"

ATTRACTIVE COMMUNICATION
CHAPTER 6
COMMUNICATIVE GIFTING

What I refer to as *communicative gifting* is the act of communicating something that will be perceived as thoughtful or valuable—without demanding anything in return. What makes *communicative gifting* attractive? People appreciate getting gifts without feeling any obligation. Yet, most often, they reciprocate by giving gifts in return.

When we think of gifting, we usually think of giving things. However, there are several kinds of intangible *communicative gifts* that attract positive responses. Among them are *information gifting*, *recommendation gifting*, and *care gifting*.

With *information gifting*, we give others information that matters to them. We should first seek information that helps them improve their health, finances, relationships, spirituality, and/or other areas in their lives. We should then communicate this information as *communicative gifts*. The more we gather helpful information and gift it to others, the more gifts we will receive in return, and the more rewarding our interactions become—both socially and in business.

With *recommendation gifting*, we communicate to others our willingness to vouch for them by recommending them to significant people in their lives. Recommendations can be personal or business in nature. If we show a genuine willingness to vouch for others, they will likely recommend us in return.

With *care gifting*, we communicate to others our concern and support. Sometimes we may not have relevant information or resources to help them, but we can still show that we care—a valuable gift in itself.

ACTION PLAN FOR COMMUNICATIVE GIFTING

Search for current useful information that **WAY 30** could improve the health, finances, relationships, spirituality, and/or others aspects of the life of the people you meaningfully communicate with. When you have that relevant information, freely give your *information gifts*. When you do, you could say something like this:

"I want to share this ___ (article, book, video, seminar, etc.) that I think might interest you."

"I want to give you this great information I found regarding _____. It will help you _____."

"You may find _____ useful because _____."

WAY 31

Give genuine *recommendation gifts* whenever possible. For example, you could say something like this:

"I would like to recommend you to _____ as a way to help you _____."

"I would be more than happy to make a call to _____ on your behalf."

"You've got my vote on _____."

"I will put in a good word for you with _____."

WAY 32

Give *care gifts* whenever possible. You may not always be in a position to give *information gifts* or *recommendation gifts*, but you can always show your concern. For example, you could ask or say something like this:

"Is there anything at all I can do to help you with _____?"

"Please know that I support you in your efforts to _____."

"No matter what happens with _____, I will be there for you."

"Please know you are important to me."

ATTRACTIVE COMMUNICATION
CHAPTER 7
COMPLIMENTS

As a source of communicative attraction, compliments are powerful. When we compliment others, we focus on the goodness we see in them. Compliments show appreciation for and acknowledgment of another person's goodness.

For compliments to be truly attractive and have a positive effect, they must be *genuine*. The appreciation we show must authentically celebrate the good in others. If we actually feel jealous, for example, then our compliments fall flat. Others would be able to notice, through our non-verbal communication (such as a fake smile or lack of eye contact), that we are not being genuine.

It is best to let go of our egos and understand that elevating others doesn't mean bringing ourselves down. When we praise others, we can build rapport and create a meaningful connection with them. That way, as they feel elevated, so do we. People who feel jealous struggle to compliment others because of their state of feeling unnecessarily

COPYRIGHT 2012 PUBLISH INTERNATIONAL, LLC

competitive. But if we consider ourselves to be on the same team as others, our compliments to our teammates actually become a compliment to ourselves as well. After all, we are on the same team!

For compliments to be attractive and have a positive effect, they must also be *realistic*. Realistic compliments highlight qualities that do exist now or have the potential to exist in the future. We should not exaggerate or fabricate facts because exaggerations and fabrications create confusion and mistrust.

ACTION PLAN FOR COMPLIMENTS

WAY 33 Actively search for anything you can genuinely compliment others on—and do it promptly.

Compliments might include:

"I hold you in high regard because _____."

"I respect you because _____."

"I admire what you did when you _____."

"I admire _____ about you."

"I think it's honorable how you _____."

"You look great."

"You have a great personality."

"What you are wearing is classy and elegant."

"I love what you have done with your home."

"I love what you have done with your office."

"You have great taste."

Avoid jealous thoughts. If you can get on the **WAY 34** same team with others, their happiness will make you happy.

WAY 35 Give compliments that are both *genuine* and *realistic*.

Attractive Communication
Chapter 8
Congratulations and
Special-Day Greetings

We can often establish attractive rapport with others by simply congratulating them on their accomplishments and special moments. People will typically feel receptive to us when we take the time to learn about their successes and acknowledge the days that are meaningful in their lives. This is because they will see us as people who care about them. Once they feel acknowledged and cared for, they will likely reciprocate and care about us.

We all know of some people who don't enjoy the successes of others. When they hear about others' accomplishments, they think about themselves and complain, saying, "Why don't I have that?," or "Aren't I as good as that person who got promoted?," or "I deserve that award instead," and so on. This kind of negative thinking often shows up in fake smiles and other unattractive non-verbal communication. Its roots are in unnecessary competition rather than cooperation. It is based on exclusion rather than inclusion, jealousy rather than self-confidence, and arrogance rather than kindness. This negative thinking is quite unattractive and polarizing. Conversely, when we genuinely celebrate the success of others by wholeheartedly congratulating them, we attract others to us.

Action Plan for Congratulations and Special-Day Greetings

Actively seek details about special moments and accomplishments of anyone you **WAY 36** currently have or would like to have personal or business interactions with. Genuinely share in those special moments, offering warm and kind congratulations for their accomplishments and special moments.

WAY 37 Find out and record birthdays for anyone you have or would like to have personal or business interactions with. Send them personalized birthday cards and/or find imaginative ways to say "Happy Birthday" on their special day.

Send holiday greetings with personalized cards every year to anyone and everyone whom you **WAY 38** have or want to have in your life.

WAY 39 Send flowers, gift baskets, or thoughtful gifts as often as possible.

ATTRACTIVE COMMUNICATION
CHAPTER 9
SMILES AND HUMOR

What's the first thing we typically hear when someone takes our photograph? "Smile!" That is because a *genuine* smile has extremely attractive properties that people want to preserve and treasure.

When we smile with sincerity, we transmit a visual image associated with kindness, warmth, happiness, approachability, and trustworthiness. When we frown, we transmit an image associated with coldness, sadness, anger, discomfort, and discontent. While a smile attracts others, a frown makes them want to run the other way.

It often takes fewer muscles to smile than it does to frown. So let's decrease our workload and engage in this attractive form of communication—smiling—as much as possible.

It is important to reiterate that only genuine smiles promote attractive communication. A fake smile is actually perceived as unattractive because it's associated with mistrust, jealousy, improper motivations, and lack of sincerity.

In addition to smiling, using humor when communicating is attractive in a number of ways. First, it gets people's attention. People like to be entertained and naturally gravitate toward whatever entertains them. Second, using humor typically causes people to laugh and relax. Someone who is relaxed is more physically capable of understanding the messages we are communicating. Third, using humor can make messages more memorable, thus elevating the retention of the content of our communications. We tend to remember things that make us laugh. Fourth, many people associate a humorous person with creativity and the arts, which are often perceived as attractive.

There are three types of humor, however, that do not promote attractive communication. First, humor that is perceived as tasteless can actually turn people off to the content of our communication. The tastelessness may in fact become associated with the content of our communication. Second, humor that is completely unrelated to the content of our communication can dilute our message. Finally, excessive use of humor in certain forms of serious communication can reduce our credibility as speakers.

ACTION PLAN FOR SMILES AND HUMOR

Smile as often as possible; change your frowns to smiles.

WAY 40

WAY 41 Smile with your face but from your heart.

Incorporate tasteful humor in your communications often. Whenever possible, relate your # WAY 42 humor to the content of your communication. Don't overdo the humor during serious forms of communication.

Attractive Communication
Chapter 10
Excitement

Excitement has a contagious energy that makes it attractive. The more excitement we communicate, the more others will be receptive to and attracted to our communications. Three important types of communicative excitement include what I refer to as *content excitement, delivery excitement,* and *associative excitement.*

Content excitement is excitement generated by uniqueness, allure, relevance, and believability. Unique content gives listeners something new—something a little different from what they have heard or read before. Even if the subject is, by most accounts, intrinsically boring, it should at least have one unique element. Alluring content attracts the listeners by posing interesting questions. Relevant content excites the listeners by promoting their goals or desires. Believable content makes it attainable. When listeners perceive what is being communicated is based in reality and lies within their reach, they become more excited about it.

Delivery excitement communicates to others that we are indeed thrilled about what we are communicating. It shows we believe in what we are conveying. Passion in the delivery of our message begets passion.

Associative excitement links the content of our communications to events, people, or things the listeners find exciting. Once that happens, listeners may be inclined to think that if a person they admire or respect likes something, then that something must be great. Listeners may also be inclined to think that if a respected company or organization uses something, then that something must be great.

ACTION PLAN FOR EXCITEMENT

WAY 43 Communicate with excitement. While some topics are, by nature, inherently unexciting, just about every communication about every subject *in this world* can have a unique and/or interesting element. Find that unique and interesting element and communicate it! See if you can pose any interesting questions.

Make your communications relevant and WAY 44 believable by conveying the attainable benefits of what you are communicating as they apply to your listeners.

WAY 45 If you do not show you believe in what you are communicating, your listeners simply will not get excited. Reveal your passion through your delivery by being dynamic and upbeat. Show people how excited you are and tell them how important the subject is to you. For example, you could say something like this:

"I'm so excited about_____ because _____."

"_____ means so much to me because _____."

"Here's what's really great about _____."

"I'm so happy to be sharing _____ with you because _____."

Find out "who" and "what" the people you are communicating with are excited about. # WAY 46
Thereafter, if you can establish a connection with those exciting people or things, you can likely achieve *associative excitement*. To do that, for example, you could say something like this:

"_____ is really excited about this; will you try it, too?"

"This would mean so much to _____; will you help me with it?"

"What I propose is similar to _____ that you are so excited about."

ATTRACTIVE COMMUNICATION
CHAPTER 11
CONFIDENCE WITHOUT ARROGANCE

Confidence communicates having ability without attaching any form of exaggeration; arrogance communicates having ability in an exaggerated way. Expressions of ability are attractive; exaggerations are not.

Confidence communicates having respect for oneself and also respect for others; arrogance communicates self-absorption and an attitude of superiority. Acknowledging oneself and others is attractive; an attitude of superiority is not.

Confident people are open to new ideas from others. They show a willingness to improve. They don't claim to be perfect. In contrast, arrogant people believe they are always right and always have the best ideas. Openness is attractive; a closed mind is not.

People often associate confidence with feeling secure within oneself and arrogance with feeling insecure. Security is attractive; insecurity is not.

ACTION PLAN FOR CONFIDENCE WITHOUT ARROGANCE

WAY 47 Do not *overestimate* others. Be confident and never allow others to intimidate you.

Do not *underestimate* others. Sometimes those you are communicating with are more WAY 48 skilled and savvy than you give them credit for.

WAY 49 Do not underestimate yourself. Believe in yourself, and communicate your confidence using words that express your ability and non-verbal communication such as standing tall and making eye contact.

Do not overestimate yourself, and, irrespective of your abilities, do not look down on others. WAY 50 Instead, treat everyone in your life the way you want to be treated.

WAY 51 Feel free to express yourself, but also be open to the thoughts and ideas of others. Communication is about the exchange of ideas.

Attractive Communication
Chapter 12
Beneficial Ambition without Greed or Envy

What I refer to as *beneficial ambition* is a type of ambition that is constructive, productive, and non-threatening. When we communicate *beneficial ambition*, we communicate our desire to act, innovate, and/or produce not only for our own benefit but also for the benefit of others. People will be attracted to our *beneficial ambition* because it is productive and non-threatening.

Conversely, communication that entails greed and envy is communication that is threatening to others. A person who communicates greed will be perceived by others as being a self-absorbed individual who is likely to "walk over" the rights of others without regard for ethics or fairness. An envious person does not celebrate the success of others and instead wants to snatch it away.

As an example, a manager who is interviewing applicants for an assistant manager position will be attracted to a passionate and driven individual who communicates that he would like to succeed by bringing value to the management team. However, the same manager will likely be turned off and/or threatened by another passionate and driven applicant who communicates solely about his or her need for self-advancement and promotion.

As another example, a man named John meets his friend Kevin's new girlfriend, Lisa, for the first time. Lisa is wonderful and amazing. If John communicates his happiness for Kevin and Lisa (as a couple) and expresses his genuine best wishes for their success together, he may end up building a solid friendship with both Kevin and Lisa. Later, if John, after having been a good friend, expresses to Lisa that he too has ambition and motivation to meet a wonderful and amazing lady, Lisa is likely to introduce him to her wonderful and amazing friends. However, if John communicates with Kevin and Lisa with greed and envy and tries to steal Lisa away from Kevin, he would most likely be regarded as disrespectful and threatening. Lisa would most probably not want anything to do with John and would not be inclined to introduce a person like John to any of her girlfriends. Kevin would likewise most probably not want anything to do with John.

ACTION PLAN FOR BENEFICIAL AMBITION
WITHOUT GREED OR ENVY

Communicate your ambitions. However, ambition is attractive to others only when it **WAY 52** is perceived as beneficial, innovative, productive, and inclusive. If the people you communicate with believe you are threatening and/or self-absorbed, they will run the other way fast!

WAY 53 Work *with* people and not *against* them. Celebrate the success of others and wish for their happiness. If you communicate greed and envy, you will isolate yourself. Greed and envy are both polarizing and destructive to personal and business relationships. Get ahead in your personal life by communicating friendship. Get ahead in business by communicating your desire to provide goods and services that make the lives of others better. Make your ambitions and passions work for others, not against them.

ATTRACTIVE COMMUNICATION
CHAPTER 13
COMMUNICATION TYPE
CONGRUENCE

People generally develop a specific communication type or combination of communication types. Ordinarily, we can determine the communication type or types by simply listening to others and observing their interactions. What I call *communication type congruence* is the skill of communicating in harmony with the communication type of those we are communicating with. When our communications are *type-congruent*—that is, the same types communicating with each other— they become more attractive, familiar, understandable, and connective than if they are not *type-congruent*.

These seven types of communicators are likely to have strong receptivity to *communication type congruence*: *Reasoners, Feelers, Lookers, Hearers, Artist-innovators, Extroverts*, and *Introverts*.

Reasoners give and receive communication best that includes logic and/or reason. For best results, communication with *Reasoners* should align with explanations, procedures, and order. The more our communication entails elements of reason, the more attractive it will be to the *Reasoner.*

Feelers communicate and respond favorably to communication that includes feelings. For best results, communication with *Feelers* should be congruent with feeling sensations. The more our communication entails elements of feeling sensations, the more attractive it will be to the *Feeler.*

Lookers give and receive communication that includes seeing, visualizing, and imagining. For best results, our communication with *Lookers* should be related to sight. The more our communication entails visual elements, the more attractive it will be to the *Looker.*

Hearers communicate and respond more favorably to communication that includes words and sounds. For best results, communication with *Hearers* should be congruent with hearing sensations. The more our communication entails elements of sound, the more attractive it will be to the *Hearer.*

Artist-innovators give and receive communication that entails expressions of originality. For best results, communication with *Artist-innovators* should be congruent with uniqueness. The more our communication entails references to creativity, the more attractive it will be to the *Artist-innovator.*

Extroverts communicate socially, enjoy interacting with others, and seek acceptance of others. Communication with *Extroverts* should be congruent with desirable social interactions. The more our communication entails social elements, the more attractive it will be to the *Extrovert*.

Introverts communicate with preferences of solitude. Communication with *Introverts* should be congruent with an *Introvert's* need for time and space to think things over with little interaction. The more our communication entails elements of patience, time, and space, the more attractive it will be to the *Introvert*.

ACTION PLAN FOR COMMUNICATION TYPE CONGRUENCE

Determine the communication type(s) of the people you communicate with. **WAY 54**

WAY 55 Communicate in a manner that is genuinely congruent with the communication type(s) of those you are communicating with.

Communicate with *Reasoners* by saying something like this: **WAY 56**

"This is the basis for _____."

"This seems logical/reasonable because _____."

"I want to tell you the theory behind this so you understand why ___ is happening."

"This is the procedure and application for this _____."

"This is good because it's consistent with _____."

"I am sure we can be rational as we decide on _____."

WAY 57 Communicate with *Feelers* by saying something like this:

"I am having a good feeling about this _____."

"This _____ just feels right to me."

"I am connected to your feelings about ___ on this issue."

"I get a good vibe from you."

"I want to connect to your feelings."

Communicate with *Lookers* by saying something like this: # WAY 58

"This looks great."

"I want to show you something."

"I want to paint a vivid picture for you about _____."

"Here is a chart and diagram for your reference."

"I see _____."

WAY 59 Communicate with *Hearers* by saying something like this:

"This is great; listen to how this sounds."

"I hear what you're saying."

"I'm really tuned in to what you are saying about ____."

"I get your message loud and clear."

"What you are saying about _____ is music to my ears."

"This really rings a bell with me."

Communicate with *Artist-innovators* by saying something like this: **WAY 60**

"This _____ is artistic."

"This _____ is a great idea—a new, original, unique approach."

"This _____ is imaginative and groundbreaking."

"This _____ is different from anything I have ever come across."

WAY 61 Communicate with *Extroverts* by saying something like this:

"We're working great with each other on this _____."

"I'm enjoying brainstorming this _____ with you."

"I would enjoy meeting you for lunch to talk about this _____."

"We should all get together to discuss _____."

"I think the group would love this _____."

Communicate with *Introverts* by saying something like this: **WAY 62**

"Take your time and think this over _____."

"I would like you to have the space you need for _____."

"Feel free to get back to me after you consider my request about _____."

"I will leave you alone now."

WAY 63

Do not use communication type congruence with destructive communication types. For example, the communication type of the *Overly Aggressives* is extreme aggression. For *Manipulators*, the communication type involves manipulation and control. For *Doubters*, the communication type entails doubting everything they see and hear. For *Egoists*, the communication type entails arrogance. When destructive communication types like these are at play, the principle of congruence is not attractive because congruence would unfortunately bring about more of the same negative types of communication.

Attractive Communication
Chapter 14
Verbal, Non-Verbal, and Mode Matching

Matching verbal communications, non-verbal communications, and modes of communications with those of the people we communicate with elevates the attractiveness of our communications. *Verbal matching* matches our words, phrases, and language patterns with those of the people receiving our communications. When communicating with others, if we include a few of the favorite words, phrases, and language patterns of the people we communicate with, our communications become more familiar and attractive.

Non-verbal matching matches our body language, intonation, distancing, and touch with those of the people we communicate with. As we communicate non-verbally, if we use similar body language, intonation, distancing, and touch as the people we communicate with, our non-verbal communications will seem more familiar and comforting.

Communication modes include in-person meetings, phone calls, instant messages (texts), emails, facsimiles, letters, video conferencing, messenger delivery, web pages, social networks, blogs, and/or combinations of these. However, the people we communicate with typically have communication mode preferences. They may prefer one or a combination of communication modes listed above. *Mode matching* matches our own mode of communication with the preferred communication mode used by those we communicate with. Although we may be inclined to automatically use our own preferred mode(s) of communication, it is important to adopt the other person's favorite mode of communication when it differs from ours. *Mode matching* brings about familiarity, comfort, and convenience for the people we communicate with and therefore makes it easier for them to be receptive to our communications.

ACTION PLAN FOR VERBAL, NON-VERBAL, AND MODE MATCHING

Listen to the words, phrases, and language patterns of the people you communicate **WAY 64** with. Include some of those in your own communications. For example, if the person often uses the word "amazing," incorporate the word "amazing" into your communications with him or her. If he or she uses the phrase "think outside the box," then incorporate the phrase "think outside the box" in your communications with him or her. If he or she uses chronological language patterns such as "first this happened, second, third, etc.," include similar chronological formats when communicating with him or her.

WAY 65

Do not match words, phrases, or language patterns in your communications that might be offensive.

WAY 66

Do not match words, phrases, or language patterns that might be grammatically incorrect.

WAY 67

Observe the non-verbal communications of the people you communicate with, then include some of the same non-verbal communications in your own non-verbal communications when they are receiving your communications. For example, if they lean forward when emphasizing a fact, you could also lean forward for emphasis. If they vary their tone when making an important point, vary your tone accordingly when you make an important point. If they prefer to have a two-foot personal space zone when communicating with you, then maintain that two-foot personal space zone. If they "high-five" you when they are happy with you, then "high-five" them when you are happy with them. However, do not overdo *non-verbal matching*; it has to be used in moderation.

Use the communication mode that the **WAY 68** person you are communicating with prefers (if it differs from yours), not the communication mode that you prefer. For example, if the person you are communicating with loves the Internet and is "tech savvy" but considers phone calls to be "unnecessary interruptions," your emails, texts, and social network posts are more attractive modes of communication to use than the phone with that person. However, if the person you are communicating with prefers to talk things out audibly instead of through the Internet, your emails, text messages, and social network posts could be regarded as impersonal and/or inconsiderate.

ATTRACTIVE COMMUNICATION
CHAPTER 15
ATTRACTIVE QUESTIONING

Questioning comes in many different types. Questioning types perceived as ineffective or unattractive include compound questioning, vague questioning, controlling questioning, inaccurate questioning, or disrespectful questioning. They should be avoided. By comparison, several types of questioning actually elevate the quality of our communications. Attractive questioning includes these six types: *open-ended questioning, positive-imaginative questioning, reflective-clarifying questioning, opinion questioning, modifying questioning,* and *apologetic questioning.*

Open-ended questioning encourages people to freely share their observations, feelings, thoughts, explanations, suggestions, and other commentary.

Open-ended questioning includes these examples:

"What are your observations?"

"How does this make you feel?"

"What are some of your thoughts?"

"What suggestions do you have?"

"I'm interested. What else do you want to talk about?"

Positive-imaginative questioning invites imagination. This form is attractive because it encourages people to imagine and experience appealing aspects of what we want to communicate. More than that, *positive-imaginative questioning* guides and encourages others to reach conclusions we want them to reach on their own. By allowing others to reach their own conclusions, this type of questioning is respectful, inviting, inclusive, and attractive, not domineering and controlling.

Positive-imaginative questioning includes these examples:

"Will you imagine _____ and share your thoughts?"

"Would you consider _____ and tell me what you think?"

Reflective-clarifying questioning entails a reflection of what we have heard, along with a request for clarification. Seeking clarification is different from making judgments. People are not attracted to judgment by others. However, they will be attracted by our efforts to genuinely understand them.

Reflective-clarifying questioning includes these examples:

"I hear you saying _____, correct?" "Please clarify _____ for me."

"I understand you to be saying _____. Is that true?" "Please tell me more about how this affected you."

Opinion questioning is a type of questioning that encourages others to express their opinions. By encouraging others to express their opinions, we will likely be regarded as open-minded, cooperative, and respectful. Once people feel that we care about their opinions, they are more likely to care about our opinions.

Opinion questioning includes these examples:

"What are your opinions about _____?"

"What feedback do you have for me?"

"How can we improve _____ together?"

Modifying questioning is a type of questioning that changes the nature of negative communication directed at us. It serves to transform negative statements by others into positive, productive questions by us. For example, if someone says to us, "You're being cheap" (because we didn't want to spend money for something), we could respond by asking, "What I understand you want to know is why I believe this expenditure isn't necessary, correct?" Using *modifying questioning*, we set the stage for a productive discussion about whether the expenditure is necessary rather than contribute to an atmosphere of negative personal attack(s).

Apologetic questioning communicates our openness to the idea that we may have been wrong. This form is attractive because it communicates candor, concern, and a desire to make things better.

Apologetic questioning includes these examples:

"I was wrong about this, wasn't I?"

"I could have done this differently, couldn't I?"

"Maybe next time I can try_____ instead of _____?"

ACTION PLAN FOR ATTRACTIVE QUESTIONING

WAY 69
Avoid asking compound questions (questions with multiple parts) within a single question. When you ask a compound question, you might be confused by the answer if it's not clear which part of your question the answer is responding to.

Do not ask vague questions. Be clear in what you are asking. Make sure all your questions are understood.

WAY 70

WAY 71
Limit your use of close-ended questions that call for a one-word or one-phrase response. Too much close-ended questioning limits the opportunity of others to freely communicate their observations, feelings, thoughts, explanations, suggestions, or other commentary. You will end up with less information, and your questions might be regarded as controlling.

Limit your use of leading questions. If you are perceived as trying to "over-control" the

WAY 72

conversation and/or are perceived as "putting words in people's mouth," you risk getting people angry.

WAY 73
Anytime your question includes a reference or a statement, make sure it is accurate. When you include inaccurate commentary in your questioning, you lose credibility.

Do not ask questions that include disrespectful comments.

WAY 74

WAY 75
If you are negative in your questioning, then the reaction and/or response to your questioning will likely be negative. Keep a positive tone and turn to attractive forms of questioning, as appropriate.

That includes *open-ended questioning*, *positive-imaginative questioning*, *reflective-clarifying questioning*, *opinion questioning*, *modifying questioning*, and/or *apologetic questioning*.

ATTRACTIVE COMMUNICATION
CHAPTER 16
ATTRACTIVE FEEDBACK

When we give feedback to others, we are communicating our observations. Feedback can be unattractive and therefore unproductive, or it can be attractive and therefore productive. The most attractive feedback consists of beneficial intentions, non-personal observations, specific observations, specific solutions, honesty, timeliness, positive acknowledgments, self-feedback, mutuality, and privacy considerations.

First, it's best to give feedback only when we have genuinely beneficial intentions—when we truly intend to be helpful and productive without ulterior motives. Feedback designed to genuinely benefit others is attractive and transmits a positive energy. Conversely, judgmental, debasing, and/or self-serving feedback is highly unattractive and can make people run the other way.

Second, our feedback is best directed at actions and not at people. An attack on a person usually leads to defensiveness. It brings about confrontation and hurt feelings. If our observations are non-personal, they will be much better received.

Third, our feedback is more helpful if it offers specific observations. For example, telling others we like their presentations is not nearly as helpful as spelling out specific reasons why we like their presentations.

Fourth, our feedback is more helpful when we offer potential specific solutions whenever possible. Most people are more receptive to feedback coupled with potential solutions rather than feedback without solutions. If we cannot provide solutions, providing a "road map" should at least be considered.

Fifth, being honest in our feedback makes a difference. If we give others false feedback, they may end up acting on false information. Not only does this hurt others, but we also hurt our own credibility.

Sixth, timely feedback is important. If we give feedback in an untimely manner, we may potentially deprive others of its benefit when it is needed most. Moreover, as time goes by, the urgency and memory of our observations decline. Unlike fine wine, feedback does not get better with age.

Seventh, our feedback is more attractive if it contains positive acknowledgements. People are interested in getting recognized for what they have done right and don't want to hear only what they have done wrong. We should look for and communicate not just the bad but also the good.

Eighth, our feedback should include a "self-feedback" element. This is when we invite those receiving our feedback to make observations of their own actions, inactions, performance, and ways to improve. Often, through "self-feedback," the people we communicate with recognize things we didn't see or think of ourselves. Moreover, because they thought of the feedback points themselves, they are much more likely to comply.

Ninth, feedback should include mutuality—that is, we do not want others to feel as though only they can improve. Every one of us can improve in what we do. If we invite people to give us feedback as well, we foster feelings of balance and fairness.

Tenth, it is important that we respect the privacy of others when giving feedback. People have an image and ego they want to protect—consciously or subconsciously. They do not want the whole world to know what they did wrong. The more we respect the privacy of people, the more they will be receptive to the substance of our feedback and the less they will be concerned about looking bad in front of others. Moreover, the comfort we provide by safeguarding their privacy encourages them to express more facts. As more information comes in to us, the quality of our feedback is enhanced.

ACTION PLAN FOR ATTRACTIVE FEEDBACK

Before giving any feedback, ask yourself about your own real intentions. If you **WAY 76** want to do anything other than be productive and serve a beneficial purpose, then it might be best to not communicate any feedback at all. Giving feedback is not a proper means of proving your superiority. Do not use the words "I told you so" or "I was right" when giving feedback to others.

WAY 77 Typically, people don't want to be judged, so making personal attacks is likely to backfire. Comment on actions, inactions, or things you observe instead. For example, rather than say, "You are a careless report writer," say something like this:

> "This report would be better if it were checked for accuracy and included more detail."

Make your feedback as specific as possible. For **WAY 78** example, simply telling others their reports are "good" is not very helpful. Instead, communicate specific reasons why you like the reports, pointing out the strong elements. That way, those receiving your feedback can apply the same strong elements to their future work. Similarly, it is not very helpful to tell others their reports are "bad." Instead, convey specific reasons why you think the reports could be better, pointing out the weaknesses. That way, in the future, they can avoid those weak elements.

WAY 79
When giving feedback, point out solutions, not just problems. Think about suggested solutions in advance, organize your thoughts, and communicate them clearly. Treat them as "proposed" or "potential" solutions rather than as mandates. For example, instead of stating they must do a specific thing, say something like this:

"I propose that you try doing _____ to solve the problem."

"Here are a few potential solutions for your consideration going forward."

WAY 80
It is very important to give feedback that is honest. Dishonesty hurts others and hurts your own credibility as well. If the subject matter is sensitive, then be "sensitively honest" but honest nevertheless. In the long run, the benefits of the trust created through honest communications far outweigh any short-term perceived burdens.

WAY 81
Give feedback in a timely manner. Once you are ready to communicate your thoughts and observations, do it as soon as possible before it's forgotten or diluted.

Before giving any negative feedback, first communicate your positive observations. **WAY 82**
This allows you to cushion the effects of your negative comments. If you cannot think of a single positive observation or acknowledgment, at least consider saying something like this:

> "I appreciate that you are here so we can work together and make things better."

WAY 83 Ask others to conduct a "self-feedback." For example, you could ask questions like these:

> "What are your thoughts about the ways you can improve _____?"

> "Have you thought about any alternatives to _____?"

> "I invite you to provide me with your own observations about _____."

Ask those who received your feedback to comment on your observations. Communicate that you value their participation and input. **WAY 84**

WAY 85 Make every effort to give negative feedback only in private.

ATTRACTIVE COMMUNICATION
CHAPTER 17
RESPONSIVE RESPONSE

When others ask questions, they are often attempting to obtain information that is important to them. We should be responsive when responding to questions posed to us. Answering questions responsively is attractive because responsive answers convey an acknowledgment and understanding of the questions. Responses that are non-responsive—that don't relate to the question asked—can create tension and confusion, making them unattractive.

Many people attempt to avoid questions or alter answers because they think their genuine answers won't be well received. However, the function of responding to a question is to reveal our genuine thoughts. If we alter our thoughts and opinions based on how we perceive they will be received by others, then we are not genuinely communicating. Our credibility will indeed suffer as a result.

There are times when we can appropriately decline to respond to certain questions. When questions seek private, sensitive, or confidential information, we can respectfully decline to provide answers. However, the principle of expressing our thoughts in a genuine manner still holds. If we think a question calls for answers that are private, sensitive, or confidential, we could respectfully say so. If we instead give inaccurate answers, we will hurt our credibility.

Another exception to responding responsively relates to rhetorical questions. Even though rhetorical questions may take the form of a question, they are not in fact genuine questions but are more like statements or declarations. We are not typically expected to answer rhetorical questions with a responsive response.

ACTION PLAN FOR RESPONSIVE RESPONSE

Refrain from answering a question with a question. **WAY 86**

WAY 87 When you are asked a question, do not be evasive. Rather, answer it as responsively and accurately as you can.

If you think the question being asked of you is highly private, sensitive, or confidential, instead **WAY 88** of giving a false or inaccurate response, you could, if applicable, respond as follows:

"I won't respond to your question because answering it goes

against my promise to keep it confidential. If circumstances change, I would be happy to answer your question."

You could also say something like this:

"I feel your question is highly private at this time. However, I am willing to revisit the issue at a later time."

WAY 89

Rhetorical questions are not genuine questions. Ask the people communicating with you if there are specific questions that they would like you to answer.

Attractive Communication
Chapter 18
Apologies and Forgiveness

As humans, we all make mistakes. Our communications can hurt others. Likewise, the communications of others can hurt us. Because hurt feelings can interfere with communication, the better we deal with the hurt, the more attractive our communications will be. Knowing how to apologize for our mistakes and being open to forgiving others for their mistakes is therefore important.

Some people say that apologies send signals of weakness. However, genuine apologies actually send powerful signals of strength. When we genuinely apologize, we demonstrate that we have a balanced ego, we have the ability to reason, and we have the ability to compromise and cooperate. These abilities are highly attractive.

We should apologize, whenever possible, in a manner that is not only genuine but also restorative—that is, we should attempt to restore what we might have taken from another such as dignity, pride, or property. If restoration is not feasible, our apology at least should communicate an intention to not commit similar hurtful acts in the future.

When we forgive, we begin the process of healing ourselves. As a result, the weight on our shoulders becomes lighter and lighter. Forgiving others can be difficult, but we can do certain things to make forgiveness easier. First, before we forgive, we can respectfully vent our hurt and frustration. A polite, non-combative expression of our feelings may help us feel better.

Second, we can assess whether another's apology is sincere by asking that person why he or she made a mistake. The information obtained will help us determine the sincerity of the apology (or lack thereof).

Third, we can forgive with a condition that the mistake made must not be repeated ever again. This allows us to communicate that although we may forgive, we will not forget.

Fourth, we can forgive with a condition that the person seeking forgiveness must restore whatever he or she has taken, if at all possible.

ACTION PLAN FOR APOLOGIES AND FORGIVENESS

Regard an apology as a sign of strength, not weakness. A genuine apology opens closed **WAY 90** lines of communication and builds bridges by manifesting reason, openness, a balanced ego, compromise, and cooperation.

WAY 91

Conduct a quality control check on yourself regularly. Ask if there is anything that you did (or failed to do) or said (or failed to say) that might have been hurtful or inappropriate. If so, promptly apologize to everyone involved.

WAY 92

If you genuinely believe you did nothing wrong, do not apologize. However, at least express that you are sorry to see those affected have been hurt or burdened. Communicate that you had no intention to hurt them and that you sincerely hope they feel better.

WAY 93

Remedy the damage you caused and restore what you can. If restoration is not feasible, at least communicate your heartfelt commitment to not repeat the act that caused you to apologize in the first place. Say something like this:

"I promise to never _____ because I don't want to ever hurt you again."

WAY 94

Turn to forgiveness as soon as possible to begin the healing process for everyone involved. When forgiving another is particularly difficult, politely and respectfully express your emotions. Carefully observe the person apologizing to you and assess his or her level of sincerity and understanding. Watch for both verbal and non-verbal signs of sincerity and understanding. Seek specific restorative action or at least satisfactory promises as conditions of your forgiveness.

Attractive Communication
Chapter 19
Best Wishes
and Encouragement

When we express our best wishes and/or encourage others, we generate positive energy and a feeling of unity and rapport. Positive energy makes our communication and its content more attractive to others. We can communicate our general best wishes by saying something like this:

"I hope you're having a nice day."

"I hope you're doing well today."

"I wish you a great day."

"I hope you're enjoying this beautiful evening."

"I hope you have a great weekend."

"I wish you a happy Monday."

We can communicate specific best wishes by first finding out the specific significant upcoming events in the lives of those we are communicating with and then conveying best wishes. We could say, for example, something like this:

"Good luck on your job interview."

"I hope you ace your exams."

"We wish you a speedy recovery from your injury."

"I hope your meeting goes well."

In addition to communicating our general and specific best wishes, we can express encouragement as often as possible in ways that follow.

First, we can encourage others by conveying our support for them. People make strong connections with those who support them. We can communicate support by saying something like this:

"I'm rooting for you."

"I'm on your side."

"I'm dedicated to your success."

"Your happiness is important to me."

Second, we can communicate encouragement by elevating the confidence of the people we communicate with. We do so by conveying the strengths, talents, and attributes we appreciate in them. We can say something like this:

"I have always respected your intelligence."

"You have a beautiful heart."

"I admire your character."

"I think you're very good looking."

Third, we can communicate encouragement by expressing hope to others who are experiencing tough times. For example, we might say something like this:

"You can do anything you set your mind to."

"Things will work out in the long run; they did for me when
_____."

"Hang in there and don't get discouraged."

"This is a temporary setback; it too shall pass."

ACTION PLAN FOR BEST WISHES AND ENCOURAGEMENT

WAY 95
Incorporate best wishes and encouragements in your communications whenever you can.

Make yourself aware of significant events in the lives of the people you communicate # WAY 96
with. Take every opportunity to wish them well at these times.

WAY 97
Genuinely encourage others, as often as possible, by providing support, elevating their level of confidence, and/ or elevating their level of hope.

ATTRACTIVE COMMUNICATION
CHAPTER 20
INTACT COMMUNICATION BRIDGES

At times, we can feel so frustrated with certain individuals that we want to cut off all ties and never talk to them again. In those moments, we can say things that could harshly end all current and potential future interactions with them.

It could be true that certain individuals are not a match for us in our personal or business lives. However, we do live in a small and dynamic world. Those people could change; the circumstances could change; our feelings could change. Moreover, they could be in our future business or social circles, or circles of friends or family. That is why communicating attractively is important, even with people who are not a good personal or business match for us.

The most appropriate communication would enable us to maintain a bridge of communication over time. If we keep our bridges of communication intact, we can choose to be in touch in the future—

or not. However, when we "burn our bridges," we generally lose something of great value; we lose our future options and choices; we reach a point of no return. The problem with reaching a point of no return is that there is no return!

There are a number of ways that we can burn our bridges. They include using exaggerations, absolute statements, and insults. Exaggerations communicate unattractive messages that we are overreacting to the situation. Absolute statements imply that we are not willing to be objective or open-minded. Insults communicate unattractive messages that we are disrespectful and/or arrogant.

ACTION PLAN
FOR INTACT COMMUNICATION BRIDGES

When you do not want further personal or business involvement with another person, **WAY 98** still keep your communication bridges intact. You do not know what the future holds.

WAY 99 Refrain from overdramatic, exaggerated, or insulting communication.

Instead of absolute statements, use statements such as these: **WAY 100**

"We are currently not a match."

"Things aren't working the way we would like for now."

"We can revisit the possibilities in the future."

PART II:

NON-VERBAL COMMUNICATION

ATTRACTIVE COMMUNICATION
CHAPTER 21
ATTRACTIVE NON-VERBAL
COMMUNICATION

Non-verbal communication, which is communication without words, is nevertheless a very important part of our communications. There are ten important ways that we can communicate non-verbally: *Eye contact, facial expressions/movements, body language, posture, gestures, mannerisms, paralinguistics, proximity, haptics,* and *non-verbal matching.*

Eye contact establishes trustworthiness and credibility in both business and personal communications and therefore is attractive. Conversely, if we look away when talking to others, they may suspect that we are hiding something. When doing presentations, we use eye contact to engage and attract our audiences. Conversely, if we don't maintain eye contact, people in our audiences might feel ignored and their attention may wander.

Attractive Communication

Our most attractive *facial expressions and movements* communicate caring, agreement, interest, attentiveness, warmth, and/or excitement. Attractive expressions include smiling, laughing, nodding the head, and more. Conversely, frowns and angry facial expressions can make people run the other way.

Our most attractive *body language* communicates caring, attentiveness, and approachability. An example is leaning slightly forward to listen. Conversely, crossing our arms, putting our feet on the table, or speaking with our backs turned to someone is often perceived as unattractive and/or disrespectful.

Our most attractive *posture* communicates confidence and includes walking tall and erect. Conversely, a slouching, slumping posture can indicate feelings of inferiority, negativity, disinterest, or lack of excitement.

Gestures such as waving are attractive only when used in a balanced way. If we do not use any gestures, we come across as dry and boring. Conversely, using too many gestures may be considered distracting. A gesture like pointing at things is generally okay. However, people typically don't like anything pointed at them, so it's best to refrain from pointing.

Mannerisms or habits such as burping, farting, picking our noses, and talking with food visibly in our mouths are obviously unattractive. However, biting our nails, tapping our pens, or the like, might also be considered distracting and unattractive as well.

Paralinguistics primarily refers to the tone, volume, and speed of vocal communication. People often regard monotone communication as dull and boring. In contrast, tone variation can be dynamic and engaging. Being too loud vocally is often regarded as rude, lacking class, or even obnoxious, while being too quiet is often regarded as lacking confidence or knowledge. People often feel rushed or confused when they hear very fast vocal communication and often get bored when they hear very slow vocal communication.

Proximity entails being considerate of another's distance and personal space. If we get too close to people's personal space, our proximity to them might seem unattractive. In fact, it could be construed as an invasion of their personal space. However, if we stand too far away from people, our lack of proximity could be regarded as distant, disconnected, and unattractive. We can often determine the most attractive distance to maintain by observing the distance that is being maintained with us.

Haptics refers to non-verbal communication by touch—something that can strengthen relationships when done appropriately. A handshake between people doing business can build rapport. A "high-five," a hug, or a pat on the back between friends can manifest support. Holding hands with a partner can communicate love, romance, and/or support.

Non-verbal matching is the process of matching our non-verbal communications with our verbal communications. If our words match our non-verbal signals, then we demonstrate consistency. However, if we say one thing and our facial expressions, for example, communicate a different message, our communications become confusing, untrustworthy, and therefore unattractive.

ACTION PLAN FOR ATTRACTIVE NON-VERBAL COMMUNICATION

WAY 101 Use eye contact to communicate attentiveness, trustworthiness, and credibility.

Smile often and nod your head as a WAY 102 means of communicating attentiveness and interest. Avoid negative, angry facial expressions. If you feel negative energy and/or anger, do your best to calm down before beginning or resuming your communications.

WAY 103 As a means of showing your attention and caring about what is being communicated to you, lean slightly forward from time to time. Avoid crossing your arms, putting your feet on the table, or speaking with your back turned to the people you are communicating with.

Walk tall and erect to exude confidence. WAY 104 Avoid slouching and falling into a weak slumping posture.

WAY 105 Use gestures to make your communications more dynamic. However, avoid using too many gestures and/or hand signals, which can become distracting. Also avoid pointing your fingers or any objects at the people you are communicating with.

Watch your mannerisms or habits. As much as possible, avoid biting your nails, WAY 106 tapping your pen, or fiddling in general. Even if you have a habit that isn't objectively objectionable, if it annoys the person you are communicating with, stop doing it.

WAY 107 Use varying tones to make your communication more dynamic. Monitor the volume of your voice so it isn't too loud or too soft. Make sure the speed of your vocal communication isn't too fast or too slow.

Do not stand too close to the people you are communicating with, nor too far WAY 108 from them. To get an indication of the right distance, observe how much space the person you are communicating with maintains with you. When in doubt, follow that same distance!

WAY 109
Touch has power. In professional settings, you can touch others in the form of a handshake. In personal interactions, use hugs, "high-fives," pats on the back, or hand-holding as appropriate.

Make sure your verbal and non-verbal communications are consistent so you # WAY 110
can avoid confusion and lack of trust.

ATTRACTIVE COMMUNICATION
CHAPTER 22
VISUAL IMAGE

We all communicate a visual image to others. Our visual image affects the perception of others. Because perception affects reality, a change in the perception of our visual image may very well become a change in our communicative reality. In other words, when we make a good impression, we elevate the attractiveness of our communication. When we make a bad impression, we negatively affect the attractiveness of our communication.

In order to establish and/or maintain an appropriate visual image, our visual image should be compatible with our message. For example, if we are offering professional services, financial services, consulting services, legal services, insurance services, or the like, it is important to convey a professional visual image. If we are offering design, music, or fashion-related services, it is important to convey an artistic visual image. If we are offering athletic training, it is important to convey an athletic visual image. If we are offering products for clear and healthy skin, it is important to show our own clear and healthy skin. Some argue that "wearing a suit or having professional stationery has nothing to do with the quality of services being offered," or "it doesn't matter if we look physically fit as long as we can teach physical training," or "not having our own clear and healthy skin does not mean that the skin products we are selling do not work." Those arguments, although potentially plausible, ignore the incredible power of visual perception and the fact that people do in fact make decisions that are based on their visual perception.

If your visual image is highly compatible with the content of your communication, it will strengthen and fortify your message, making your communication more attractive. Conversely, if you are communicating a message that does not match your visual image, you can create confusion and even mistrust.

ACTION PLAN FOR VISUAL IMAGE

WAY 111 Match your visual image with the substance of your communication.

Make sure your visual image does not exaggerate nor understate the substance of your communication. WAY 112

PART III:

COMMUNICATION TIMING AND SURROUNDINGS

ATTRACTIVE COMMUNICATION
CHAPTER 23
APPOINTMENTS

We live in a busy world. Whether we operate in a personal or business environment, setting aside a specific time to communicate is of utmost importance. Having appointments or "time allocations" helps make our communications more effective and attractive for the following six reasons.

First, when we take time to set an appointment with another person, it doesn't get forgotten easily. People tend to write down (or otherwise remember) their appointments, thus increasing the odds that the communication will in fact take place.

Second, making appointments gives us quality, uninterrupted time to communicate our message and/or accomplish our goals. Each appointment typically entails one-on-one communication at a set time, thus eliminating a need to compete for the time and attention of the person we are communicating with.

Third, setting an appointment acknowledges the importance

of other people's time and schedule. When we respectfully request a "time allocation," we signal a preference to *coordinate* with that person rather than *interrupt* him or her. Acknowledgment begets acknowledgment.

Fourth, having an appointment affords us time to prepare for it, which in turn gives us a chance to refine the content of our communications. This enhances the *quality* of our communications.

Fifth, having an appointment likewise affords others time to prepare. They appreciate having time to gather information before discussing the subject at hand. They also invest their time and thought into the subject, which leads to attaching greater importance to the communication that is to take place.

Sixth, appointments deter *positional attachments. Positional attachments* take place when others get attached to a position they were rushed into. If we rush others to formulate an opinion, they might quickly come up with positions that go against our wishes. It is much harder to change a position than it is to keep the same position from forming in the first place.

ACTION PLAN FOR APPOINTMENTS

WAY 113 When communicating an important message or making a meaningful request, ask for a meeting or appointment.

Make the meeting or appointment as convenient as possible for the other

WAY 114

person to minimize interruptions and maximize his or her focus.

WAY 115

Communicate the amount of time you will need for the meeting or appointment. Build in a time "cushion" so you can engage in a meaningful, reasoned exchange of ideas on any issues that arise without being rushed.

Thank the other person for cooperating and allocating precious time for mean-

WAY 116

ingful communications with you.

ATTRACTIVE COMMUNICATION
CHAPTER 24
SURROUNDINGS

Our surroundings influence the attractiveness of our communications. This is true both in business and in personal communications. Attractive surroundings align with the preferences of the people we communicate with and with the content of our communications.

For example, if we want to have an important business lunch with a client who likes fine dining, we should make a reservation at the restaurant he or she chooses, even if it is not our number one preference. That way, the client feels comfortable with the menu, the staff, the ambience, and so on. By increasing his or her comfort level, we will heighten his or her receptivity to our communications.

If we want to communicate important messages to a romantic interest, then we should make sure the surroundings are romantic and beautiful. Romantic settings set the mood for romance. Our efforts in creating a romantic and attractive setting, will surely enhance the attraction to our communications.

If we want to communicate important messages to friends who like music, we should take them to a restaurant that features the kind of music they prefer. That way, they will enjoy the music and be happy, appreciative, and more receptive to what we have to say.

Conversely, surroundings that harm communication are filled with distractions. For example, if the people we are communicating with do not like crowds, we should avoid meeting in crowded locations. As another example, if the messages we want to convey are private, we should avoid places where lots of friends and acquaintances go.

ACTION PLAN FOR SURROUNDINGS

WAY 117
When selecting a place to communicate important messages or requests, convey consideration of and respect for the people you communicate with. Focus on the preferences of the people you communicate with.

Match your surroundings with the content and substance of your communications.

WAY 118
For example, romantic communications should take place in romantic settings. Private communications should take place in private settings.

WAY 119
Make reservations at your meeting place so that the people you are meeting with feel you have made an effort.

WAY 120
When meeting in your house or office, place drinks, sweets, and/or healthy snacks within reach of the people you are meeting with. Food and drinks often make many people feel happy.

WAY 121
When meeting in your house or office, make sure your surroundings are neat and orderly. If the people you are meeting with observe sloppiness, or lack of organization, they may feel that you are a sloppy or disorganized person.

ATTRACTIVE COMMUNICATION
CHAPTER 25
PUNCTUALITY

Punctuality means more than arriving on time; it communicates trustworthiness, competence, and dependability. These are all attractive qualities. Conversely, if people believe we can't keep our time commitments, they might assume that we are unable to keep other commitments. Moreover, if they think we don't care about being on time, they might infer that the subject matter of our meeting is not important to us.

Punctuality communicates interest in and respect for everyone participating in the meeting. Conversely, if we keep people waiting, they might feel as if we are not motivated or that we are rude.

Returning phone calls promptly and meeting reasonable time expectations of others are also important aspects of punctuality. The failure to do these things can communicate lack of trustworthiness, lack of competence, lack of interest in the subject matter, and/or lack of interest in and respect for the other person.

ACTION PLAN FOR PUNCTUALITY

Maintain a calendar that you have access to at all times.

WAY 122

WAY 123
Mark every appointment on your calendar.

Avoid setting up an appointment at a time that you are not sure about.

WAY 124

WAY 125
Allocate enough time to get to your destination without unnecessary stress.

Incorporate a time "cushion" in all your appointments.

WAY 126

WAY 127
To deal with times when you are late due to events beyond your control, take these actions:

As soon as you realize your lateness, promptly and respectfully call those you are meeting and tell them you could be late.

Briefly explain the unexpected delay.

Apologize for being late.

If the people you are meeting appear to still be upset about your tardiness, promise to make it up to them.

Return all phone calls by the end of the **WAY 128** calendar day or, without fail, no later than 24 hours from the original call. If you cannot do that for any reason, ask someone else to call within 24 hours on your behalf to advise that you will soon be calling.

WAY 129 Meet all reasonable time expectations as set forth by the people you are communicating with. If you think any requests are unreasonable, don't commit to them. Instead, respectfully suggest alternatives.

ATTRACTIVE COMMUNICATION
CHAPTER 26
GOOD MOODS

As emotional beings, we are affected by our moods. People have feelings that range from bliss to extreme sadness. The best time to communicate with another person is as close as possible to the time of that person's bliss—and as far away as possible from the period of his or her extreme sadness. Why? Because good moods provide for a greater level of openness and receptivity to the messages we communicate. Bad moods elevate the chances that our communication will not be attractive or effective.

It can be frustrating having made an appointment in an appropriate surrounding, yet the person we're meeting with is in a bad mood. However, that's a reality of life. When the other person is simply not ready, willing, or able to receive our message, we have to reschedule our meeting despite the inconvenience. As we reschedule, we should communicate our wishes that they "will feel better" and assure them that "everything will be alright." It's important to convey genuine caring and understanding and to show empathy instead of complaining or getting angry. This caring and understanding can go a long way in our rapport with the person we are communicating with.

At times, we might not know the mood of the person we intend to communicate with. To gain insight, we can look for "non-verbal signs." These may include visual, auditory, or other signs that show how the person may be feeling. Visual signs may entail a lack of eye contact or a look of fatigue, frustration, or boredom. Auditory signs may entail an angry or depressed tone of voice. Touch signs may include lack of touch or "pushaways." Distancing signs may include the person walking away or not inviting us in. When we cannot discern the non-verbal signs, we can simply ask people if they are in a good mood. People appreciate it when we show our interest pertaining to how they feel.

ACTION PLAN FOR GOOD MOODS

As part of your communications, assess the moods of the people you **WAY 130** communicate with. A good mood generally means a much higher receptivity to your communications than a bad mood.

WAY 131 Look for *non-verbal mood indicators.* For example, look for manifestations of happiness versus sadness, relaxation versus stress, enthusiasm versus boredom, focus versus lack of attention, closeness versus distance, etc.

If, after observing the people you are **WAY 132** communicating with, you are not sure about their moods, then just ask. For example, you can ask something like this:

"How are you feeling?"

"Is this a good time to discuss _____?"

WAY 133 If the moods of the people you are communicating with are marginal, offer mood enhancers. For example, you can go out for coffee, lunch, or desserts.

If the moods of the people you are **WAY 134** communicating with are not good, and you are not in a position to enhance the moods, then consider rescheduling your meetings. Rescheduled communications are better than bad communications! You can ask something like this:

"Given how you feel, would you prefer to reschedule our meeting to another date?"

ATTRACTIVE COMMUNICATION
CHAPTER 27
PATIENCE

One moment of lack of patience could result in "putting our feet in our mouths." It can cause lasting damage to our relationships with others. Conversely, being patient could elevate the attractiveness of our communications in a number of important ways. Patience shows that we care about others and that we are ready, willing, and able to let them share their feelings and thoughts with us in a meaningful way. The more others feel heard and understood, the more they will reciprocate and be open to the content of our communications. Moreover, patience enhances the quality of our own communications with others. It gives us the opportunity to think carefully before we speak—to consider, analyze, and refine the content of our communications.

Patience also encourages others to consider their own positions and/or points of view. It affords them time to think and talk things through. By doing that, they may even reach the conclusions we want them to reach all on their own.

By practicing the skill of patience, we gain better rapport, clearer content for ourselves, improved content from others, and ultimately a more attractive communication.

ACTION PLAN FOR PATIENCE

WAY 135 Take the time to listen and think before you speak. Choose your words carefully. What you say can and will be used against you.

When deciding if you should rush your communication or push for a decision WAY 136 from another, consider the costs versus the benefits of doing so. Is the time you save by *not* being patient worth sacrificing rapport? Is it worth lowering the quality of the content of your communications? Is it worth instigating a negative response?

WAY 137 Plan for patience and incorporate it into your communications as a means of quality control. How would you feel about taking medication, or eating food, or driving a car whose producers made no effort to control quality? The same concept applies here. Communications without any quality control often turn out to be poor and/or risky.

When waiting for an important decision, think of "patience time" as a gift of time. Relax and do something you find interesting.

WAY 138

Attractive Communication
Chapter 28
Brevity

Brevity—the art of communicating effectively without taking too much unnecessary time—is attractive for reasons including the following three.

First, brevity communicates respect. Most people have busy lives and value their time. When we communicate in a way that shows respect for others' time, we gain respect and receptiveness in return.

Second, brevity communicates competence. When we properly focus on the main issues, we show that we understand. We show that we "get it."

Third, brevity makes the content of our communications memorable. People have a limited attention span. If we communicate too much information, we can create "information overload," making that information hard to remember.

ACTION PLAN FOR BREVITY

WAY 139
Specifically show that you respect the time of others by saying something like this:

"I appreciate and value your time."

"Out of respect for your time, let me get right to the point."

Focus more on communicating what you do want rather than what you don't # WAY 140
want. That will save you time and get to the heart of the matter. For example, you would not go to a bookstore and tell the owner about the 100 books you don't want. You would order the book you do want. At a restaurant, you would tell the food server the few items on the menu you do want, not the 50+ items you don't want. Simply get to the point when communicating. When you focus on what you want, you are practicing brevity.

WAY 141
Avoid information overload. Break down long, complicated issues into small, manageable parts, and exclude content that's irrelevant or unnecessary.

Avoid vague and confusing language. Use simple, clear expressions instead. # WAY 142
Save flowery language for discussing literature.

WAY 143

Just as the amount of sculpting materials used does not necessarily make a great sculpture or the amount of paint used does not necessarily make a great painting, the quantity of words used does not equate to the quality of communication. Limit the quantity of your words to what is necessary.

WAY 144

Consider using acronyms to cut down on recurring references. An acronym is a word formed from the initial letters of other words. For example, if you will be referring often to Mothers Against Drunk Driving, use the acronym MADD.

PART IV:

LISTENING

Attractive Communication
Chapter 29
Participatory Listening

An integral part of communication is listening. The most attractive and effective communications involve what I refer to as *participatory listening*, which requires participating physically, mentally, and emotionally in the listening process.

Participatory physical listening entails hearing with our ears the words being communicated to us as well as observing with our eyes the non-verbal messages of the people communicating with us. To enhance our hearing, it is best not to interrupt. After all, we can't hear others if we interrupt them. The best way to observe non-verbal messages is to actually look for them. If we do not make a point to observe others' non-verbal communication, it will be difficult to put their words into proper context.

Participatory mental listening requires the understanding of the events, conditions, or facts that form the basis of what is being communicated to us. Moreover, it requires that we clearly understand what the people communicating with us want.

Participatory emotional listening consists of caring about the people who communicate with us. Our ears can hear information; our eyes can pick up non-verbal clues; our minds can process information. However, it is in our hearts that we truly feel what the people communicating with us are feeling.

ACTION PLAN FOR PARTICIPATORY LISTENING

WAY 145 Do not interrupt others when they are talking.

Do not finish the sentences of others when they are talking. # WAY 146

WAY 147 Look with your eyes for non-verbal messages while listening.

Mentally focus on understanding the events, conditions, or facts that form the # WAY 148 basis of what is being communicated to you. Also, find out exactly what the people communicating with you want. Moreover, make sure that you understand the feelings of the people who are communicating with you.

WAY 149 As you listen, avoid thinking about your own responses.

As you listen, refrain from thinking about matters unrelated to what is being communicated to you. # WAY 150

WAY 151 Do not compare yourself with the people talking to you while you are listening to them.

Do not guess what the people talking to you are thinking while listening to them. # WAY 152

WAY 153 As you listen, refrain from judging the people who are talking to you.

ATTRACTIVE COMMUNICATION
CHAPTER 30
LISTENING MANIFESTATIONS

It's important not only to participate in the listening process but also to attractively manifest or express to others that we did so.

The manifestation of *participatory physical listening* consists of communicating to others that we hear them. We can say, for example, "What I hear you saying is," followed by the words the person just stated. This provides proof that we took in the words spoken to us.

The manifestation of *participatory mental listening* consists of communicating to others that we understand them. We can say, for example, "I understand you to mean," followed by what we understood the substance of their message to be. This provides proof that we understood the point, essence, message, and/or meaning of what was communicated to us.

The manifestation of *participatory emotional listening* consists of validating or acknowledging the feelings and emotions of others. For example, we might say something like this:

"You must be feeling _____."

"I acknowledge your emotions."

ACTION PLAN FOR LISTENING MANIFESTATIONS

After listening carefully, communicate what you heard as closely as possible **WAY 154** to the way you heard it. With long conversations, it is appropriate to paraphrase.

WAY 155 Communicate clearly and succinctly your understanding of what is being communicated to you. If you have questions, seek clarification.

If the people you are communicating with are asking for something, convey **WAY 156** your understanding of what they want.

WAY 157 Acknowledge the feelings of the people communicating with you.

ATTRACTIVE COMMUNICATION
CHAPTER 31
ATTRACTED LISTENING

Attracted listening is a type of listening that communicates an eagerness and enthusiasm for the communications of others. The more we show our attraction to the communications of the people we communicate with, the more they will be attracted to our communications.

Before we manifest attracted listening, it is important to first get attracted to what is being communicated to us. If we are simply not interested, then our lack of enthusiasm will show. Attracted listening must be genuine to be effective. At those critical moments when we are starting to lose interest in what is being communicated to us, we should immediately try to elevate our interest. One way to do so is to keep an open mind and reserve judgment. It may get better and more interesting as we continue to listen.

Another way is to think long-term rather than short-term. For example, in business, even though one particular transaction is boring or unprofitable, if we build rapport in the process of doing that transaction, we can enjoy great long-term future profits. By reframing the boring transaction as a profitable "rapport-building" transaction, we can elevate our attraction to it.

As another example, our romantic partner might at times want to talk about something we have no interest in. However, even though the discussion may be boring, if we build intimacy by continuing to care and listen, then we can enjoy the long-term benefits of a close and intimate relationship. By reframing the boring discussion as an "intimacy-building" discussion, we can elevate our attraction to it.

Even when we are engaged in a boring discussion with people whom we have no business or personal relationship with, maybe we can simply enjoy helping them by allowing them to feel heard, understood, and comforted. Helping others in a time of need can itself very much serve as an attractive, worthwhile endeavor.

Once we elevate our inner attraction to what is being communicated to us, we should then show it. We can do so by using words of support, responding with *positive flow responses*, taking notes, asking questions, and using non-verbal manifestations.

ACTION PLAN FOR ATTRACTED LISTENING

Elevate your attraction to the content of what is being communicated to you. **WAY 158** Keep an open mind and reserve judgment. Moreover, think "long-term," not "short-term." Remember, the way you listen can significantly affect your relationships with the people communicating with you. It can also affect their feelings and well-being.

WAY 159

After you have elevated your attraction to what is being communicated to you, use words of interest to manifest attracted listening. For example, you might say something like this:

"What you are saying is very interesting."

"I want to learn more about the subject you are talking about."

"This is a great conversation."

"I'm happy to be discussing this matter with you."

"I'm interested in hearing and understanding you."

WAY 160

Use words of support. For example, you might say something like this:

"I believe in your abilities."

"I think you're really making an effort. Way to go!"

"I invite you to continue to share your thoughts about _____ with me."

WAY 161

Use what I refer to as *positive flow responses*, which are words that keep the conversation flowing and show you are interested. They include expressions such as "I see" or "oh wow" or "interesting" or "tell me more."

Take notes as often as possible to show the people communicating with you that **WAY 162** you are engaged and interested in what they have to say.

WAY 163 Use non-verbal manifestations such as an open/inviting posture and facial expressions showing focus, enthusiasm, and/or surprise. Maintain eye contact, smile, nod your head, lean toward the people communicating with you, and so on.

Do not rush the communication of the people communicating with you. It **WAY 164** indicates you want to hurry up and finish the conversation. It can also indicate you aren't interested in what they have to say.

WAY 165 Ask questions to indicate your interest in learning more about what is being communicated to you.

If you are listening in a group, do not conduct side conversations. Side conversations imply you are not happy with the main conversation. **WAY 166**

ATTRACTIVE COMMUNICATION
CHAPTER 32
SPEAKER-FOCUSED LISTENING

M any of us listen to others speak with a focus on ourselves, our needs, and our interests. Although attention to self is important, when it comes to listening, a self-focus orientation can be unattractive and ineffective. Conversely, what I refer to as *speaker-focused listening* (concentrating exclusively on the speaker) is powerfully attractive for numerous reasons, including the three that follow.

First, *speaker-focused listening* improves concentration. The purpose of listening is to hear and understand what other people are saying. If we focus on ourselves while listening, we have less of our attention available to grasp what is being communicated to us. Conversely, if we completely focus on the people communicating with us, our entire attention becomes available to the listening process. Moreover, the people communicating with us will be able to observe and appreciate that we are giving them our undivided attention.

Second, *speaker-focused listening* allows us to let our egos take a break. It allows us to momentarily free ourselves from defending and/or from proving ourselves. It is no longer about us. In fact, it has nothing to do with us. Instead, it is solely about the speaker and his or her communication. As we become less defensive, we experience an energy shift *away from* confrontation and *toward* cooperation and collaboration. Letting our egos take a break also allows us to work *with* others and not *against* others. Consequently, we become more open to what is communicated, which makes it attractive for others to share more information with us. Ultimately, we learn more and become more effective listeners.

Third, *speaker-focused listening* encourages *speaker-focused listening* by others in return. Once the people communicating with us observe our substantial effort to understand what they have to say, they will be encouraged to reciprocate and will try harder to understand what we have to say. Once others perceive that we are listening cooperatively and not defensively, they in turn will give their own egos a break and work *with* us, not *against* us.

ACTION PLAN FOR SPEAKER-FOCUSED LISTENING

WAY 167 When listening to others, do not think about your own goals, interests, or desires. Listen exclusively to hear and understand the content of what is being communicated to you. Concentrate on gathering as much information as possible so you can fully understand the goals, desires, and interests of the people talking to you.

Put aside any urge to jump in and defend # WAY 168
yourself, even if you strongly disagree with the content of what is being communicated to you. You will later get a turn to both defend yourself and to communicate additional information you deem appropriate. Defending yourself at the wrong moment will only break up the flow of information to you, interfere with your concentration, and possibly create unnecessary contention.

WAY 169
Encourage, respect, and validate those you are talking to by showing them you are completely focused on them. You might say something like this:

"You have my complete attention."

"You have the floor."

"I'm focused on completely understanding you."

ATTRACTIVE COMMUNICATION
CHAPTER 33
NO-SOLUTION LISTENING

Many of us have been taught to be problem solvers. As we listen, we are often determined to find a solution to a problem or to give feedback. Many times, that is exactly what the people communicating with us want. They want our opinions and proposed solutions. They want feedback. However, sometimes the people communicating with us have needs that are more important than opinions, solutions, or feedback. In these circumstances, *no-solution listening* may be more attractive and effective than solution-oriented listening.

A *no-solution listening* approach is appropriate when those communicating with us want to vent and release hurtful emotions after getting upset. They are not seeking advice. When they are distressed and emotional, our efforts to "problem-solve" are not practical. They simply want someone to talk to and share their feelings with. They want to be heard. They want to be understood. They want empathy from us.

A *no-solution listening* approach can also be appropriate when the people communicating with us want to find out if they can trust us. In such cases, they do not necessarily want our expertise. Rather, they seek to discern if we can be a confidant. In personal relationships, it can be a test of intimacy.

No-solution listening can also be appropriate when the people communicating with us are, at the moment, feeling low on self-esteem or confidence. It is not a time to judge but a time to give comfort. It is a time to communicate that we believe in them.

No-solution listening can additionally be appropriate when those communicating with us are too tired to engage in a solution-oriented, analytical dialogue. The resolution of certain issues requires substantial effort and concentration by everyone involved. If the people communicating with us feel tired, it will be difficult to have a meaningful exchange of ideas. In fact, our efforts in being helpful in an analytic way could backfire and add to their frustration.

ACTION PLAN FOR NO-SOLUTION LISTENING

If the emotions underlying the communications directed to you are too **WAY 170** strong to allow for a meaningful exchange of ideas, first convey your empathy and understanding. Instead of interrogating, judging, or giving recommendations, respectfully reflect back what you understand the emotions of the people communicating with you to be. For example, you could say something like this:

"As I understand it, you seem very upset about _____."

"It seems like you're feeling disappointed in _____."

"It must have been difficult for you to learn that _____."

"I can certainly understand how you could feel hurt about _____."

WAY 171
When you notice that the people communicating with you are reaching out to confide in you and are evaluating whether they can trust you, communicate your trustworthiness. For example, you could say something like this:

"I trust you and want to reassure you that you can trust me, too."

"I will hold what you tell me in confidence."

"I am here for you and will keep our talk confidential."

WAY 172
When the people communicating with you make statements that suggest they are lacking confidence, communicate the things you appreciate about them. For example, you can say something like this:

"I believe in you."

"I know you always come through."

"I appreciate how you handled _____ in the past."

WAY 173

When the people communicating with you seem too tired to have a productive dialogue with you, let them finish talking without interruption but ask to continue the conversation later. You might ask, "What you're saying is very important to me. Can we continue this conversation tomorrow so you can get some rest?"

ATTRACTIVE COMMUNICATION
CHAPTER 34
NO MULTITASKING

Multitasking may have very limited benefits in certain areas of our lives. However, in the field of communication, multitasking is incredibly unattractive and detrimental. I refer to multitasking during personal or business communications as *communicative multitasking*. *Communicative multitasking* may entail routinely taking phone calls during a conversation, typing away on the computer during a conversation, listening to music in the middle of a conversation, watching television during a conversation, instant messaging or texting during a conversation, thinking and/or paying attention to unrelated topics during a conversation, etc. When we engage in *communicative multitasking*, we convey underlying messages that are not intended but which nevertheless result in negative perceptions by others. Three negative perceptions associated with *communicative multitasking* follows.

First, many people may feel a lack of importance. They may think, "I must not be important enough to have an uninterrupted conversation with this person." Second, many people may feel the content or subject of their communication is not being well received. They may think, "I guess this person is not interested in what I am talking about." Third, many people may feel disrespected. They may think that "this person is rude and disrespectful and should learn some manners." All of these negative perceptions/feelings/thoughts are highly unattractive.

Conversely, if we focus and concentrate exclusively on listening to the person communicating with us, we bring about attractive perceptions of us. Others will likely perceive us to be attentive, focused, diligent, cooperative, interested, caring, and respectful—all attractive qualities.

ACTION PLAN FOR NO MULTITASKING

Refrain from multitasking while communicating with others. **WAY 174**

WAY 175 If you have an emergency that requires your attention, apologize and communicate that you have an emergency to attend to. Express your desire to resume your communication at your earliest opportunity.

If you are unable or unwilling to give your undivided attention to the people you are **WAY 176** communicating with, reschedule the communications. Rescheduled communications are much better than bad communications.

PART V:

PERSUASION AND DISPUTE RESOLUTION

ATTRACTIVE COMMUNICATION
CHAPTER 35
CREDIBILITY

For our communications to be persuasively attractive, we must have credibility—a very important part of persuasion. You cannot persuade people to take action effectively without it. Credibility is derived from sources including education, licensing, experience, writings, self-study, and/or association.

Educational credibility pertains to our education and the knowledge acquired through formal learning. It could include degrees we have earned, courses we have taken, and/or seminars/workshops we have attended. *Educational credibility* communicates that we have spent substantial time and effort in learning about the content of our communications. Degrees and certifications constitute sources of credibility that are verified by an independent body in charge of administering related course work and standards.

Licensing credibility refers to the licenses acquired through rigorous testing. It communicates being tested by a licensing body that certifies we have met the requirements of the licensing we acquired. Based on objective, verifiable standards, licensing is also typically conducted by independent organizations or authorities.

Experiential credibility relates to our experiences and demonstrates that we have applied the elements of our communications in practical ways. Because no objective or independent evaluation can be made of our *experiential credibility*, the level of our credibility depends on how well we communicate the value, uniqueness, and relevance of our experiences. We must show that the quantity and quality of our experiences allow us to offer meaningful opinions about the subject of our communications.

Writings credibility relates to the writing of noteworthy newsletters, trade journals, course materials, books, blogs, or other similar communications. It is often assumed that if others regard our written materials to be noteworthy, then our communications deserve consideration.

Self-study credibility is credibility that is based on our own targeted research of issues relating to the content of our communications. Having in-depth, up-to-date information as pertaining to the content of our communications elevates our credibility. The more we show that we are informed, the more credible we will be.

Association credibility has to do with being associated with industry groups, people, events, or things that are credible. The more we associate with credible groups, people, events, or things, the more credible we will be. Conversely, if we associate with people, organizations, or events lacking credibility, we ourselves can lose credibility. Stated differently, positive associations enhance our credibility while negative associations reduce it.

ACTION PLAN FOR CREDIBILITY

WAY 177 Establish credibility by communicating your relevant education, licensing, experience, writings, self-study, and associations that pertain to the content of your communications.

When communicating your credibility, be informative but not arrogant. WAY 178

ATTRACTIVE COMMUNICATION
CHAPTER 36
LIMITED AVAILABILITY OF OFFERINGS

Offers, proposals, or opportunities become more attractive if there is limited availability. Why? Because people do not want to miss out! In fact, the fear of missing out on something attracts attention and results in action. Important types of limitations on offerings include *quantity limitations, quality limitations, time limitations*, and *process limitations*.

Quantity limitations convey that if those we are communicating with do not act, they might lose the opportunity to do so in the future because quantities are limited. *Quality limitations* convey that if those we are communicating with do not act, they will miss out on the available levels of quality of the goods, services, or offerings being offered. *Time limitations* require that the people we are communicating with act promptly or they will miss out on the opportunities being offered altogether. *Process limitations* convey that if the people we are communicating with do not act promptly, they will miss out on the current process of performance of the opportunities being offered.

ACTION PLAN FOR LIMITED AVAILABILITY OF OFFERINGS

WAY 179
Communicate the limited nature of your offers, proposals, or opportunities related to quantity, quality, time, and process.

Explain to those you are communicating with that the limitations on your offerings # WAY 180
require them to act promptly. If they do not act, they could miss out on these offerings. Explain to them that time is of the essence.

WAY 181
If there is competition for your offerings, communicate the fact that others want what you are offering. By doing so, you will thereby elevate the level of urgency.

ATTRACTIVE COMMUNICATION
CHAPTER 37
VALUE COMMUNICATION

The more we communicate value, the more our offerings become persuasive and attractive. Four points to consider when communicating value follow.

First, it is important to focus value communication *more* on the needs and wants of those we are communicating with and *less* on our own. Most of us are quick to communicate why we want or need something. But people want to know what's in it for *them*. The more we focus on *their* needs and wants, the more attractive our communications become.

Second, *value communication* requires a complete discussion of the benefits being offered. Benefits can take many forms including physical, financial, social, emotional, intellectual, and more. Being complete in communicating *all* the benefits of our communications/proposals is very important.

Third, *value communication* requires a discussion of cost

avoidance. Costs can take the form of financial loss, privacy loss, time loss, opportunity loss, reputation damage, stress, and more. Being complete in communicating *all* the ways our proposals help avoid costs is very important.

Fourth, *value communication* is more attractive when it is both subjective and objective. The value we *objectively* place on our proposals could be *subjectively* perceived as being different from what we intended. Stated differently, what we value as *most* important could be viewed as *less* important by those we are communicating with. So while it is important to communicate objective general benefits and costs savings of our communications/proposals, the specific subjective/unique value allocations of the people we are communicating with cannot be ignored. It is wise to genuinely place the greatest emphasis on the benefits most valued and the costs most feared by the people we are communicating with. If we do not know what the specific subjective value allocations are, we should simply ask the people we are communicating with directly or ask others who know them. We could also research websites, writings, blogs, posted resumes, professional/social networking postings, and other public expressions of the people we are communicating with.

ACTION PLAN FOR VALUE COMMUNICATION

To be more persuasive, focus on the wants and desires of those you are communicating with. They need to know—promptly and

WAY 182

completely—how your communications/proposals can benefit them.

WAY 183
Carefully discuss all the benefits of your communications and proposals. For example, if you are offering a job to someone in great demand, don't discuss only the salary and financial benefits; also emphasize the comfortable low-stress environment, the respect and recognition you will provide, the intellectual/learning opportunities that come with the job, the social/networking opportunities associated with it, the cooperative/friendly culture of your firm, work flexibility, future growth potential, and so on. The more benefits you communicate, the more persuasive and attractive your communications/proposals will be.

WAY 184
Carefully convey all the genuine costs that might result from rejecting your proposals/communications. For example, if you have a dispute with your business partner but want to avoid litigation, point out the inevitable costs of litigation, including damage to your business/personal relationship, opportunity costs, loss of privacy, large attorney fees and court costs, unpredictability of the outcome, loss of time from work for employees called as witnesses, and so on. The more *cost avoidance value* you communicate, the more persuasive your communications/proposals will be. Make your "cost avoidance" language cooperative, collaborative, and informative—never

threatening. For example, you could say something like this:

"I want us to cooperate and collaborate with each other so we can avoid costs such as _____."

"One of my goals is for us to prevent _____."

ATTRACTIVE COMMUNICATION
CHAPTER 38
COMPARISONS AND CONFIRMATIONS

Most people take time to compare what we tell them for accuracy and persuasiveness. Specifically, they compare what we are conveying to similar things they have heard or experienced before. They compare what we are offering to various offers they have received or been aware of before.

Statements that are consistent with similar statements they believe to be true become more familiar and attractive to them. Similarly, offers that match up favorably to comparable offers become more attractive. So to increase the persuasiveness of our message, it is important to educate ourselves on relevant comparisons. That way, we can communicate three factors—*factual consistency, experiential consistency*, and *value superiority*—when discussing these comparisons.

Most people also take time to confirm what we tell them for accuracy and persuasiveness. Specifically, they confirm if what we are conveying is accepted by others and if what we are offering is viewed favorably by others. Statements accepted by others become increasingly persuasive and offers confirmed by others to be "attractive" become more attractive. So to increase the persuasiveness of our message, it is important to confirm that relevant people accept and believe in what we are saying.

ACTION PLAN FOR COMPARISONS AND CONFIRMATIONS

WAY 185 Be aware that people often compare and confirm before deciding if what you are communicating is persuasive. The more you do the comparisons and confirmations for them as part of your communications, the more familiar, believable, and attractive your communications will be.

Establish *factual consistency*. Ask the people you are communicating with **WAY 186** about statements they believe to be true. Thereafter, genuinely make your communications consistent with those statements. For example, if you are the owner of a marketing firm trying to sign up business owners as your clients, you may ask your prospects if they believe that marketing and advertising is important to their company's success. If they respond with a "yes," you have created a *factual consistency* between what they stated to be important in business (marketing/advertising) and what your firm offers. In another example, if your single lady friend feels lonely and you want her to date, you might ask if she believes love and family can be an important part of life. If she says "yes," then you establish a factual consistency when you suggest she starts dating to find a future love partner.

WAY 187

Establish *experiential consistency* by asking those you are communicating with about their relevant experiences. Thereafter, make your statements genuinely consistent with what they say. For example, if your marketing firm wants to sign up business owners as clients, you might ask if they have had any positive experience with marketing campaigns in the past. Or you might ask if they find any television, radio, or print ads in the market to be interesting. If they say "yes," then start talking about the consistencies, if any, between the services you offer and the positive experiences of the people you are communicating with. In another example, if you want your friends to start dating after bad breakups, you might ask them to recall any good relationships they may have had in the past. Even if they have never had a good relationship, ask them to think about the good relationships of people they know. You can then point out the *experiential consistency* between your suggestion of dating and the positive dating experiences that your friends are aware of.

Remember to communicate in detail all the ways your products, services, **WAY 188** offerings, proposals, or suggestions are superior to the alternatives.

WAY 189 Establish *testimonial consistency*. For example, if you are selling products or providing services, share testimonials from people who have benefited from your products or services.

Attractive Communication
Chapter 39
Examples, Anecdotes, and Quotes

When trying to persuade others, theoretical communication may not be enough. To better attract and persuade the people we communicate with, we may need to use examples, anecdotes, and/or quotes.

Examples and anecdotes (short, interesting stories) apply theories to real-life situations and therefore create familiarity. They help people better understand and remember what we are communicating. Especially when we are giving live presentations, examples and anecdotes can help raise energy and attention levels, and can help us better connect.

Quotes can be very effective if the quotes have clever and relevant messages. Moreover, if the author of a relevant quote is well known and respected, then the quote tends to create persuasion by association. In addition, quotes are usually short and to the point, making them easy for people to remember.

Action Plan for Examples, Anecdotes, and Quotes

Make sure that you are clear about the objectives of your examples, anecdotes, and/or quotes, and that your objectives are actually met. **WAY 190**

WAY 191 The examples, anecdotes, and/or quotes you use must make the content of your communications more familiar to your audience.

Make sure that the examples, anecdotes, and/or quotes that you use do not offend your audience. **WAY 192**

WAY 193 Use quotes that are relevant, clever, and meaningful. If you can find a quote from a well-known and respected person to support your contentions, you create persuasion by association.

Keep examples, anecdotes, and/or quotes short. Do not include unnecessary details. **WAY 194**

WAY 195 Refrain from using speech fillers such as "umm," "like," "uhhh," etc.

If you are speaking in public, deliver your **WAY 196** stories in a dynamic and passionate way. Remember to use pauses, intonation, gestures, and eye contact.

WAY 197 Before telling a story as part of your presentations, first practice in front of a mirror and then do a test, if possible, in front of friends/family/co-workers. Don't just communicate a boring narrative of events. Instead, give an exciting performance with characters and actions.

Make sure all your stories end in a clear **WAY 198** and powerful manner.

Attractive Communication
Chapter 40
Flexibility

Integrating flexibility into our communications can serve to elevate the persuasive attractiveness of our communications. Three ways flexibility can make our communications more attractive follow.

First, by incorporating flexibility into our communications, we essentially provide others with more choices. The more options we offer, the higher the likelihood that we will have an agreement.

Second, flexibility empowers others to be involved in the decision-making process. People like to decide which options work better for them rather than having decisions made for them. When people make decisions on their own, rather than having decisions forced on them, they become more involved and committed to carrying out their decisions because they participated in making them.

Third, people generally associate flexibility with openness, fairness, and a willingness to cooperate. In return, they will likely reciprocate and be more open, fair, and cooperative with us. Thus, flexibility begets flexibility.

ACTION PLAN FOR FLEXIBILITY

WAY 199 Be as flexible and open as possible when thinking and expressing your thoughts.

Before communicating any request to act or to refrain from taking action, offer WAY 200 alternatives that are equally acceptable to you. When you add available options, you increase the odds that one or more would be happily accepted. For example, you could say something like this:

"If _____ is unacceptable to you, consider _____ or _____ instead. Any of these options are okay with me."

WAY 201 Whenever possible, communicate your openness to the suggestions and ideas of the people you communicate with. Acknowledge their contribution and incorporate their ideas in your communications. For example, you could say something like this:

"Thank you for your input and cooperation. The following option of _____ integrates your suggestions."

ATTRACTIVE COMMUNICATION
CHAPTER 41
COMPLAINT MODIFICATION

Complaining is one of the most unattractive and negative forms of communication. It promotes contention and defensiveness, not resolution and cooperation. What I refer to as *complaint modification* entails modifying complaints to reduce complaint-related negativity in communication. Two effective ways to modify complaints that will enhance productivity and attractiveness in our communications follow.

First, we can modify our complaints by turning them into questions—a process I refer to as *complaint-question modification*. Often, we complain because we don't understand what others are saying to us, and we respond with phrases such as "you don't make sense" or "you don't know what you are talking about" or "that's crazy." These sorts of complaint-oriented communications, however, come across as fighting words. They instantly create contention and defensiveness. If we simply turn our complaints into respectful questions, we will be perceived as asking for clarification rather than asking for a fight.

Second, we can modify our complaints by turning them into requests—a process I call *complaint-request modification*. When the people we are communicating with continue to do things we do not like, many of us complain by saying, "Why do you always do this to me?," or "I'm sick of this," or "You really screwed up," or "You don't know what you are doing." However, these sorts of complaints are also perceived as fighting words, and we face resistance because of it. If we simply turn our complaints into polite requests, we can be perceived as asking for change, not a fight.

Complaint-question modification and *complaint-request modification* can serve to make the communication of others more attractive to us as well, thus promoting a more attractive response from us in return. So when we modify others' complaints and turn them into questions and/or requests to us, we comfort our own egos and decrease our own levels of contention and defensiveness. Instead of defending ourselves from complaints or insults, we shift the focus to answering questions and/or responding to requests. We go from being defensive to being productive.

ACTION PLAN FOR COMPLAINT MODIFICATION

When you want to complain, DON'T! WAY 202

WAY 203
Ask yourself why you were inclined to complain; find the source.

If you thought the other person didn't make sense, modify your intended # WAY 204 complaint into questions that seek clarification of what is being communicated to you. Your goal is to understand the points being made. For example, you could ask questions like these:

"What does this mean?"

"Why is this so?"

"How does this work?"

"Where does this information come from?"

"When does this work this way?"

You can also ask for clarifications like these:

"Tell me more."

"Please clarify what you mean by _____."

"Please give me an example or an analogy."

"Please draw a diagram of what you mean."

WAY 205
If you understand what is being communicated to you but want to change the outcome, first ask yourself what you want those you are communicating with to do or to refrain from doing. Then politely make a request. For example, you could say something like this:

"Instead of _____ , I ask that you do _____ ."

"I'd appreciate it if you would do _____ instead of _____ ."

"I respectfully request that you refrain from doing _____ ."

If others complain to you but you think they don't understand you, turn their # WAY 206

complaint into a question. Next, verify the accuracy of the question to make sure you understand it correctly. Finally, simply answer the question. For example, if you are selling your house and a potential buyer believes you are asking too much and calls you greedy, turn the insult or complaint into a question by asking something like this:

"It appears you'd like to know what it is about my house that makes it worth more than other houses in the market. Is that true?"

After verifying the accuracy of the question, then answer it. Notice a shift away from a potentially very negative argument and toward a conversation that is informative, productive, respectful, and attractive. The person who called you greedy could even end up buying your house!

WAY 207
If others complain because they want you to change something, modify their complaint by turning it into a request. Next, verify the accuracy of what you understand their request to be. Finally, respectfully respond to the request. For example, if a potential buyer of your house

complains to you that the landscaping of your house is ugly, say something like this:

"I get the sense you're unhappy with how the landscaping looks and that you would want it to be improved. Is that right?"

"If you agree to buy my house, I will improve it in the following ways so that it will be acceptable to you. Okay?"

ATTRACTIVE COMMUNICATION
CHAPTER 42
ATTRACTIVE RESPONSE

There are times when we feel that certain individuals are being very difficult, unreasonable, or uncooperative. In response, we are often very quick to make a negative comment. We may even give them a negative look or stare. However, by doing so, we often cause them to become defensive and even more uncooperative. When we respond in a negative manner, we actually breed more negativity and therefore reduce our persuasiveness, even if our negative response may have been well deserved.

In order to attractively persuade others to change, it is important that we resist the urge to respond with negative comments or behaviors. Instead, we should consider using an *attractive response*. An *attractive response* consists of verbal or non-verbal communication that is agreeable and encouraging. The more attractive our response, the more likely we are to attract the attention and receptiveness of the people we communicate with.

ACTION PLAN FOR ATTRACTIVE RESPONSE

When the people you are communicating with are being very un- **WAY 208** cooperative, try to remember instances in the past when they have been very cooperative. Attractively respond to their lack of cooperation by reminding them about the times when you were all very successful because you were all able to work with each other as a team.

WAY 209 When your loved ones are very upset and uncooperative, attractively respond by holding hands, hugging, or otherwise showing them love or affection. That will typically calm them down and encourage them to once again connect with you.

When your business partners, associates, customers, or clients are not being fair **WAY 210** with you in a transaction, remind them about the times when they have demonstrated their fairness to you. Remind them how much you have valued their fairness in the past.

WAY 211 When the people you are communicating with are making statements that are untrue, think about the times when they have been honest with you. Express to them how much you value their honest past communications with you.

Attractive Communication
Chapter 43
Repetition

When used appropriately, repetition has four attractive and/or persuasive qualities.

First, repetition helps listeners better understand our communications. Because of variances in comprehension abilities, there could be internal listening distractions we are unaware of such as the listener having a bad day or dealing with an illness. So repeating our messages allows those who missed our messages the first time to understand them a second or third time.

Second, repetition makes our communications more memorable and/or more familiar to our listeners. The more times they receive the same messages, the more they will remember them. That is why repetition is used in memory training and advertising. The first time we communicate, we create a memory footprint. The second time, we create a memory footpath. The third time, we create a memory road. The fourth time, we create a memory highway.

Third, repetition promotes a perception of importance because it has a highlighting effect. Listeners consciously and/or sub-consciously equate repetition with matters that are noteworthy. A good example is Abraham Lincoln's famous phrase "government of the people, by the people, for the people." This phrase attractively and effectively highlights the importance of the word "people."

Fourth, repetition provides opportunities to listeners to reconsider what we are saying. By repeating our communications, they are given new chances to accept our propositions after thinking about them. If initially they disagreed with our communications but later changed their minds, repetition allows them to "save face" and agree with the new repeated communications. This is because repeated communications bring about new opportunities for acceptance.

Communication can be repeated in multiple forms: repeated directly, with word variations, with anecdotes, and/or with quotations. The more we vary the form of our repetition, the more impact we will have. Form variation makes repetition more interesting.

Repetition can also be delivered using multiple modes: in person, by phone, email, fax, blog, and so on. The more we vary the mode of our repetition, the more impact we will have.

ACTION PLAN FOR REPETITION

Recognize that many people need to have the content of your communications **WAY 212** repeated before they fully understand what you are communicating. Tell your listeners what you are going to communicate, then communicate it, then tell your listeners what you have communicated.

WAY 213 Use repetition to make the content of your communications more memorable.

Use multiple repetitions to highlight major points and to communicate **WAY 214** importance or urgency.

WAY 215 If you encounter initial resistance by listeners to your communications, use repetition to create new opportunities for acceptance. You can also use repetition to *image facilitate* and to allow your listeners to "save face." For *image facilitation* or "face-saving" purposes, you need to somewhat alter your communications so that your communications are not exactly the same. The slightest modifications will provide new opportunities for acceptance.

Change the forms and modes of your repetitions often. **WAY 216**

ATTRACTIVE COMMUNICATION
CHAPTER 44
COMMONALITY

When we are in an adversarial situation, many of us jump into communicating our differences. We immediately start communicating why we are right and why others are wrong. By focusing first on our differences, we often generate a negative, polarizing energy, which in turn brings about defensiveness and resistance to our communications.

A more attractive approach is to first communicate commonality, which serves as a rapport-building foundation. From that foundation, we can build a bridge that brings us together.

These three types of commonality can elevate the attractiveness of our communications: *personal commonality, goal commonality,* and *positional commonality.*

To communicate *personal commonality,* we consider the interests, experiences, feelings, preferences, and/or values of the people we are communicating with. We then communicate what we have in common with any of these interests, experiences, feelings, preferences, and/or values.

With *goal commonality*, we consider any goals we have in common with the people we are communicating with. They could be large, medium, or small goals, general or specific. At a minimum, we all share a goal of communication.

With *positional commonality*, we consider the known positions of those we are communicating with. If we agree with any of these positions, we communicate that accordingly. If we don't quite agree, then we at least respectfully convey our understanding of the facts and opinions being communicated. We also communicate a willingness to listen with an open mind and invite those we are communicating with to do the same.

ACTION PLAN FOR COMMONALITY

WAY 217 When you are trying to resolve your differences, first communicate your commonality before communicating your differences.

Share with others what you have in common in terms of interests, exper- # WAY 218 iences, feelings, preferences, and/or values. If you don't know much about them, ask around and look for related websites, writings, blogs, posted resumes, social network postings, and other public expressions.

WAY 219

Ask yourself what goals you have in common with the people you are communicating with. Remember, at a minimum, you at least have a common goal of having a productive meeting. For example, you could say something like this:

"We are all here to have a meaningful exchange of ideas."

"We are here to work together and arrive at a mutually acceptable solution to _____."

"We have come together in good faith to try to work things out."

WAY 220

Communicate your agreement regarding any facts, opinions, or positions that you genuinely agree with. At times, you might fear being perceived as giving in or being weak by communicating agreements. However, being honest, open, and forthright actually sends a signal of good-faith cooperation, not weakness. Good-faith cooperation generally brings about good-faith cooperation in return. If the person you are communicating with doesn't cooperate, then you will at least gain valuable information about the type of person you are communicating with. If you are not sure whether you agree or not, at least acknowledge your openness to consider what is being communicated to you. You could say something like this:

"I will consider your comments with an open mind."

"I respect your efforts in sharing your thoughts and will consider everything you have conveyed to me."

Ask the person you are communicating with to likewise consider the content of your communication with an open mind.

ATTRACTIVE COMMUNICATION
CHAPTER 45
MUTUAL FAIRNESS

Unfortunately, many of us focus heavily or even exclusively on *self-fairness* rather than on *mutual fairness* in our communications. As a result, we are quick when communicating fairness that pertains to us but slow when communicating fairness that pertains to others. However, *mutual fairness communication* is far more attractive than *self fairness communication* for the following four reasons.

First, mutuality begets mutuality. *Mutual fairness communication* is about "we" rather than "me." It indicates an intention to move toward the people we communicate with and encourages others to reciprocate and move toward us. Conversely, self focus begets self focus, with self fairness being about "me" and not "we." It indicates our intent to move away from the people we communicate with and encourages others to reciprocate and move away from us.

Second, the familiar concept of mutual fairness is considered to be socially good and acceptable. At some point, almost all of us have heard from our parents, teachers, and/or mentors messages such as "Be fair to others as well as to yourself," or "What is fair is fair," or "Everyone has to be fair," or "Do unto others what you want done unto you." Conversely, "selfishness" is considered to be socially bad and unacceptable.

Third, *mutual fairness language* is generally perceived as an invitation to cooperate and collaborate rather than to confront and compete. By communicating a desire for mutual fairness, we are likely to be perceived as balanced.

Fourth, *mutual fairness language* is respectful because it acknowledges the rights of others. Conversely, many people find self-centered communication to be arrogant and/or disrespectful.

ACTION PLAN FOR MUTUAL FAIRNESS

WAY 221 When discussing fairness, communicate *mutual fairness* rather than *self fairness*.

Refrain from making *self fairness statements* such as the following: # WAY 222

"That _____ isn't fair to me."

"Doing _____ doesn't treat me fairly."

"That's not the fairness I was looking for."

WAY 223

Make *mutual fairness statements* like these:

"I want to work with you to reach a solution that's fair to both of us."

"I want what is fair for both of us."

"I want us to both be accountable for _____."

"I want us to achieve a win/win solution."

Offer to work *with* others rather than work *against* others. You could say something like this:

WAY 224

"I want to work with you and not against you."

"I invite you to work with me and not against me."

WAY 225

When the people you are communicating with appear to be too focused on themselves, ask them if they will commit to mutual fairness. You could say the following:

"Will you promise to do what you can to achieve what's fair for both of us?"

"Will you commit to mutual fairness when dealing with _____?"

"Will you work with me to achieve a resolution that's fair to everyone involved?"

Even if they are selfish or self-centered, they will almost always say they believe in—and will commit to—mutual fairness. Once they have made that commitment, they typically will feel inclined to act consistently with their commitment.

ATTRACTIVE COMMUNICATION
CHAPTER 46
REASONABLE CONCLUSIONS

Disputes are sometimes a part of our lives. As part of the process of resolving disputes, we reach various conclusions. The quality of those conclusions will indeed affect how we resolve our disputes. Therefore, it is important that we reach reasonable conclusions from the information presented to us. Reaching reasonable conclusions requires first getting all the facts. It also entails asking the right questions and covering the relevant bases. If we get incorrect or incomplete facts, we can end up with incorrect or incomplete conclusions.

Reaching reasonable conclusions also requires an objective analysis of the facts we obtain. The quality of our analysis is just as important as the quality of our facts. It requires us to be open-minded enough to consider all potentially plausible positions and explanations. If we are too judgmental, we become less reasonable, and our analysis could become too rigid and/or one-sided.

Reaching reasonable conclusions additionally requires that we have empathy as we contemplate the facts we become aware of. After all, not everyone has the same background and experiences as we do. Unique personal experiences make for unique factual explanations. If we expect absolute perfection, we are sure to reach conclusions that are not reasonable. Indeed, the only fact we can be perfectly sure of is that no one is absolutely perfect in every way!

It is not my position that we reach conclusions that are necessarily consistent with the conclusions of others. Rather, as we attempt to resolve our disputes, we should communicate conclusions that are well reasoned. Well-reasoned conclusions are attractive. Headstrong conclusions are unattractive.

ACTION PLAN FOR REASONABLE CONCLUSIONS

First, gather all the facts. WAY 226

WAY 227 Ask any questions that you may have, as pertaining to all the facts.

Make sure to consider all the information you obtained before reaching a conclusion. WAY 228

WAY 229 Be empathetic and open-minded.

ATTRACTIVE COMMUNICATION
CHAPTER 47
SWITCHING SHOES

The most attractive communications take place when there is genuine understanding. One powerful way to truly understand and to be understood is to *switch shoes* with someone else. That entails putting ourselves "in the shoes" of the people we communicate with and requesting they put themselves "in our shoes."

Putting ourselves in the shoes of the people we communicate with requires that we ask them about their observations, thoughts, and feelings. We should listen carefully and then assume that we *are* them; we observe, think, and feel as *they* do, not as *we* do. Then we specifically acknowledge each of these observations, thoughts, and feelings from the perspective of the people we communicate with.

We must first acknowledge others in order to attract acknowledgment from them. When people feel that their observations, thoughts, and feelings have been acknowledged, they are more open to stepping into our shoes. Once we have completed the process of acknowledging others, it is important to specifically and respectfully request that others put themselves in our shoes. Doing so will help them better identify with us.

ACTION PLAN FOR SWITCHING SHOES

When you are having differences and/or disputes, put yourself "in the shoes" of **WAY 230** the people you are communicating with.

WAY 231 Communicate to the people you are having differences with that you are trying to see things from their perspective.

Ask the people you are communicating with to take a moment and observe, **WAY 232** think, and feel as you do. You could say something like this:

"I invite you to put yourself in my shoes."

"I want to request that you see things from my perspective."

"I want you to see where I am coming from."

"Could you see how things could be different from my vantage point?"

WAY 233
Consider educational experiences, work experiences, personal experiences, and/or other experiences of the people you communicate with when stepping into their shoes. This will enable you to better identify with them, making it easier for you to step into *their* shoes.

If you have certain educational experiences, work experiences, personal

WAY 234
experiences, and/or other experiences that have been meaningful to you, share them so others can better identify with you. This makes it easier for them to step into *your* shoes.

ATTRACTIVE COMMUNICATION
CHAPTER 48
IMAGE FACILITATION

Most people have a public image that they exhibit. Most if not all people want their public image to be as great as it can be. They want others to hold them in high regard. They want to appear important, knowledgeable, and consistent. As we are trying to resolve our disputes, we should not be confrontational. When we "point fingers" at others and force them to accept that they are wrong, negligent, inconsistent, or unprepared, we will face a powerful resistance from their egos.

Attractive communication entails communication that does not offend the egos of the people we communicate. When we use image facilitation, we facilitate the desired image of others to remain intact. Following are five important ways we can *image facilitate*.

First, we can *image facilitate* by providing *fresh facts* for others to consider. In effect, we are creating a brand new proposition, a new equation, a new formula, a new offering. Even if others told us earlier their decision was final, their statement of finality no longer applies because we now have a new set of facts and circumstances for them to consider. Introducing new facts "unfinalizes" the decisions made and shifts others from a "boxed-in" status to a "free-to-choose" status.

Second, we can *image facilitate* by offering an *acknowledgment.* That means that before looking for ways to break down what others are saying, we seek to identify any conduct or statements that could be reasonable. We then acknowledge their reasonability. Once we have acknowledged that something the other person has said or done is reasonable, that person will have an easier time communicating to us that what we say is reasonable as well.

Third, we can *image facilitate* by offering an *alternative.* Some people may communicate firmly that they will absolutely not give us a certain thing that we are requesting. However, they might be willing to give us something else that is equally important to us. Instead of "pushing" others into a situation in which they might appear weak and/or inconsistent if they give in to our demands, we can instead pull them toward us by giving them a creative alternative to consider. Because alternatives actually create fresh new propositions, people can freely consider our requests without feeling cornered.

Fourth, we can *image facilitate* by communicating *empathy* and *understanding.* Instead of debasing others, we could convey an understanding of how they might feel the way they do. Once the focus shifts from "people being wrong" to "circumstances being understandable," any burdens on the ego are significantly cushioned.

Fifth, we can *image facilitate* by communicating in ways that will not be perceived as *boasting* or *bragging*. Other than stroking our own egos, boasting/bragging does not make our communications more attractive or effective in any manner. Instead, it fuels others to do anything in their power to prove us wrong.

ACTION PLAN FOR IMAGE FACILITATION

WAY 235 Do not point fingers at people, either literally or figuratively.

If you get a final decision, "unfinalize" it by offering new facts. For example, you # WAY 236

could say something like this:

"I understand how you might feel, but I invite you to consider the following new facts: _____."

Then explain why and how the new facts make a difference.

WAY 237 Offer acknowledgments whenever possible. For example, you could say

something like this:

"I appreciate your time and your dedication not to rush to judgment."

"You make a good point about _____. Therefore, I'm sure

you can be open to reaching a reasonable conclusion about
_____ as well."

Give alternatives. For example, you could say something like this:

WAY 238

"I understand you do not want to do _____ at this time, but please think about _____."

WAY 239
Use empathy instead of making personal attacks. For example, when applicable, you could say something like this:

"I understand you may have had incomplete information that caused you to reach the conclusion that you initially reached."

"I acknowledge that you might have obtained inaccurate information and it understandably caused you to reach the conclusion that you initially reached."

"I gather there just wasn't enough time for you to fully analyze the subject matter of our communication."

You can also couple your empathy with invitations. For example, you could say the following:

WAY 240

"I understand how you could have reached the conclusion that you did based on the information provided by others. However, here is the complete and correct information for you to consider.

I invite you to read it and reconsider your decision."

As another example, you could say something like this:

"I understand that, at this time, there hasn't been enough time for you to fully consider my requests. So I invite you to take the time you need before getting back to me with your final decision."

WAY 241
Refrain from bragging/boasting. For example, don't ever say, "I told you so," or "See, I am right; you are wrong," or "I win; you lose," or "I am better than you," or "You will never be as good as I am," or "You must listen to me because I know what I'm talking about."

ATTRACTIVE COMMUNICATION
CHAPTER 49
SUPPLEMENTAL FACILITATION

We can elevate the attractiveness and persuasiveness of our communications through *supplemental facilitation*—the process of facilitating the acceptance of our proposals/communications using procedural/supplemental incentives. Five important ways we can put *supplemental facilitation* into effect follow.

The first way is to offer a choice in the *timing* of performance. For example, a proposal might be rejected because the person we are communicating with feels rushed. We can make our proposals more attractive if we can offer choices. For example, "Clean your room immediately" is less attractive than "Clean your room by tomorrow." "If you want to settle the case today, you must pay me today" is less attractive than saying, "Sign the settlement papers today and pay me within 30 days." "I need your response in two hours" is less attractive than saying, "I need your response in two days."

The second way is to offer choice in the *method* of performance.

At times, the people we are communicating with might not be able to comply in the manner that we want them to comply. However, when we provide more options, we heighten the chances that the people we are communicating with can comply after all. For example, saying, "You must pay cash" is less attractive than saying, "You can pay half cash, and I will take a trade-in or promissory note for the other half." Saying, "Cancel your holiday tomorrow and meet me for an hour to discuss the problems with the project" is less attractive than saying, "Please set aside an hour from your holiday tomorrow morning to discuss the problems with the project."

The third way is to offer *trials/guarantees*. A trial is an opportunity to test or try out what we are proposing with less of a commitment. Offering trials shows a willingness to let others "get their feet wet" before jumping in. Depending on how we word our trials, offering them can also communicate confidence. For example, we could say something like this:

> "I have a lot of confidence in what I'm communicating, so I'm happy to extend an invitation for you to try it and see how you feel about it."

Guarantees allow others to return to the position they were at before they accepted our proposal. They also communicate confidence in our offerings while reducing risk. As such, they attract acceptance.

A fourth way is to offer *confidentiality*. The people we communicate with could have sensitivities or privacy concerns pertaining to our communications with them. By offering them confidentiality, we address their privacy/sensitivity concerns. That in turn makes our communications more attractive. For example, if we want to settle a case, we might say, "I will agree to keep the settlement terms confidential." If we want to encourage a loved one to confide in us so we can help them, we might say, "I promise to keep what you say between us and will not share it with others."

Last but certainly not least, we should try to make proposals that benefit the public or have societal value. Most people want to be part of the greater good. Many businesses increase sales and improve their brand by donating a portion of their proceeds to charities. If we genuinely care about the public good and commit to helping others as a regular part of our lives, people will notice. Generosity, kindness, and thoughtfulness are very attractive qualities.

ACTION PLAN FOR SUPPLEMENTAL FACILITATION

In advance of your communications, ask yourself if you would be willing to offer a **WAY 242** choice regarding time of performance, method of performance, and/or trials/guarantees. Offer any type of incentives that you are comfortable with to facilitate acceptance of your proposals/communications.

WAY 243 Ask yourself if any part of your communications could entail sensitive or private issues. If so, communicate your genuine willingness to keep related sensitive and private issues confidential.

Regularly think about the public good, and genuinely make altruism a part of your life and business. Altruism is attractive.

WAY 244

Attractive Communication
Chapter 50
Declining Communication

Every verbal or non-verbal message should serve the purpose of the intended communication. In other words, if we are trying to convey information, our words and non-verbal communications should be effective in conveying information. If we are trying to persuade, our words and non-verbal communications should be persuasive. If we are trying to make a request, our words and non-verbal communications should be effective in moving us closer to our goals.

However, there are times when, despite our best efforts, as we continue to communicate, we actually convey less information, we become less persuasive, and our requests are more likely to be declined. That is the point I refer to as the point of *declining communication.*

Once we reach the point at which the next point we communicate would actually diminish the effectiveness and/or attractiveness of our communication, we must stop the negativity and instead consider alternatives. Appropriate alternatives to *declining communication* include *listen-only communication, restart communication,* and *rescheduled communication.*

Listen-only communication entails shifting the focus away from conveying information, persuading, or requesting and moving it toward listening only. We should wholeheartedly listen until the people communicating with us have completely communicated their thoughts and/or vented any negative feelings they harbor. As we exclusively listen, the people we are communicating with are likely to experience a quick change in energy. The resistance to our message would be replaced with the rejuvenating feeling of being completely heard, understood, and respected. When others feel completely heard, understood, and respected, they will generally become more receptive to what we have to say. Now we can resume our own communications.

Typically, once we conduct *listen-only communication,* we are able to create the rejuvenated positive energy necessary for the people communicating with us to become more receptive. However, there may be times when the tension level is still too high to communicate effectively and attractively. If, despite our efforts, we once again experience resistance to our message to the point of *declining communication,* we might want to try restarting communication.

Restart communication entails inviting the people we communicate with to join us in simply relaxing, taking a break, and restarting or "rebooting"—much like computers that need to sometimes be restarted or rebooted.

Rescheduled communication is the best communication when *listen-only* and *restart communication* is not effective. A rescheduled communication is better than a bad communication. Sometimes it is better to stop communicating. I do not suggest that we stop forever. Rather, I suggest we respectfully request to reschedule our communications for a different time and location.

ACTION PLAN FOR DECLINING COMMUNICATION

WAY 245
If your communications are going nowhere fast and anything you say seems to negatively affect the attractiveness and effectiveness of your communications, you might be at the point of *declining communication*. Every time you communicate, know whether or not you are communicating attractively. Recognize *declining communication* and promptly take corrective action. Don't continue what is not working.

Try *listen-only* communication. Focus and concentrate on what is causing the

WAY 246

negative resistance to your communication. Gather as much information as necessary so you can later improve the attractiveness and effectiveness of your communication. Make sure the people you are communicating with feel completely heard, understood, and respected.

WAY 247

Sometimes, you may need to generate new energy by *restarting* your communication. You could say, "Let's start over," or "Let's take it from the top." You could even excuse yourself, go outside, re-enter the room, and begin a new conversation from scratch as if the unsuccessful communication never took place. Perhaps even change your location entirely. You could ask to go out for a walk or a meal— somewhere that the person you are communicating with enjoys. If you are having a phone conversation, consider inviting the person you are communicating with to start a new phone conversation in a few minutes. Ask that person to forget that the previous phone conversation ever took place.

WAY 248

After restarting your communication, if you again reach the point of *declining communication*, then you might have to *reschedule* for another day altogether. You could say something like this:

> "The communication between us is too important to rush. Let's reschedule for another day so we can give it the one hundred

percent effort it deserves."

"It seems we might be getting tired. Let's reschedule so we can be full of energy and excitement when we communicate with each other."

ATTRACTIVE COMMUNICATION
CHAPTER 51
PROMISE REQUESTING

When others make a promise, they are generally attracted to keeping their promise because they want to maintain both a positive self-image and a societal image of reliability and dependability. Most people do not want to be regarded as a "flake" or a "fake." Therefore, if we think others might explicitly make a promise to us, we should communicate a request for that promise. By getting others to make a promise to us, we elevate the chances of their compliance.

Sometimes we are not able to get an actual explicit promise, but we can get alternatives to a promise. For example, others may say they are "inclined" to do what we want them to do. Perhaps they may "predict" that they will do what we want them to do. Even though the "inclined to" and "predict" alternatives are not as strong as an explicit promise, they do increase the odds of compliance in our favor. This is because people generally do not want to contradict their own declared inclinations and/or predictions. Therefore, any time we can get an "I am inclined to" or "I predict," we should do so.

The best promises or promise alternatives are the ones that are made in writing by the promise maker. A written instrument serves to directly confirm verbal promises and is perceived as having very little "wiggle room." If it is not practical to get the promise in writing from the maker of the promise, then it would be helpful if the promise is heard by people whom the maker of the promise knows and respects. The more people who hear the promise, the more image there is to protect. Alternatively, we can consider sending a letter or email that confirms the promise, even "cc"ing others who are involved, as appropriate.

ACTION PLAN FOR PROMISE REQUESTING

WAY 249
Whenever possible, request from others an explicit promise that they will do what you want them to do. You might ask, "Do you promise to _____?," or "Do I have your word that you will_____?"

WAY 250
If you are unable to get the people you are communicating with to make an actual promise, request promise alternatives. For example, you might ask, "Are you inclined to _____?," or "Do you predict you will _____?"

WAY 251

If practical, get the promise or promise alternatives in writing from the promise maker. If not practical, see if you can have the promise overheard by people whom the promise maker knows and respects. You could also send the promise maker a confirmation letter or email, confirming the content of the promise, as appropriate.

ATTRACTIVE COMMUNICATION
CHAPTER 52
INTERIM SOLUTIONS

When we have reached a roadblock in dispute resolution, we should not give up. Rather, we should continue to communicate attractively and attempt to at least reach what I refer to as *interim solutions*. *Interim solutions* are temporary solutions designed to help us avoid escalated contention and/or litigation. Potential interim solutions include *partial agreements, conditional agreements*, and/or *status quo agreements*.

Partial agreements are designed to allow us the opportunity to at least resolve some of the outstanding issues even if we cannot achieve a complete resolution of all of the issues. Unfortunately, many of us take an "all or nothing" approach to dispute resolution. However, dispute resolution can be achieved partially. We should therefore try to resolve as many issues as possible, whether small, medium, or large.

Conditional agreements allow us to continue our efforts to resolve our disputes without having to unilaterally "bid against ourselves."

This is because *conditional agreements* are mutual by design. In other words, we would offer something on the condition of getting something in return.

Proposing a *conditional agreement* is attractive because it is based on familiar notions of fairness and reciprocity. For example, if we are $100,000 apart in our positions, we could offer to move $25,000 closer if (and only if) the person we are communicating with also moves $25,000 closer. If our condition is accepted, even though we would not resolve all disputes in their entirety, we would at least come $50,000 closer. If our condition is not accepted, then we would be back to being $100,000 apart as before. By attempting a *conditional agreement*, not only do we not lose our negotiation position, but we also communicate attractively. We send a message that we would be willing to respond to mutual effort, cooperation, and collaboration.

There are times when, at the moment, you may not be able to reach *partial* or *conditional agreements*. However, you may be able to at least agree to a form of cease-fire. A *status quo agreement*, like a cease-fire, preserves the status quo. It could take the form of an agreement not to sue each other in court for a specified period of time and/or an agreement not to escalate the current level of discord for a specified period of time. *Status quo agreements* allow us some time, space, and breathing room.

ACTION PLAN FOR INTERIM SOLUTIONS

If you are unable to resolve certain issues at the moment, do not sabotage **WAY 252** issues that you can resolve. Try to resolve as many as possible, even if they are small or merely procedural issues. Being able to resolve issues, however small, sets a positive tone for future discussions.

WAY 253 If you are concerned that the person you are communicating with is not being cooperative and you are concerned about bidding against yourself, try making *conditional offers*. You can say, for example:

> "Because I am committed to good-faith negotiation, reciprocity, and mutual cooperation, I am willing to move $25,000 closer to your number if you come $25,000 closer to my number. We can then revisit the matter at a later time in the hopes of reaching a complete global settlement."

If you cannot achieve peace, you may be able to at least get a cease-fire. Ask to **WAY 254** preserve the status quo. In personal relationships, for example, you might say:

> "So that we can all calm down and think things through, I propose that we both agree that we won't be making any negative comments to each other or to others until we meet again in a week."

In business, you might say:

"I propose that we meet in thirty days and that we do not sue each other during that time so we can continue to work with each other amicably."

ATTRACTIVE COMMUNICATION
CHAPTER 53
MEDIATION

Even when we believe that the people we are communicating with are being very difficult, we should not give up. We can still communicate attractively by respectfully requesting that we bring in a mediator to help us resolve our issues amicably. A mediator is typically a neutral third party with no stake in the outcome. A mediator's task is to help us voluntarily resolve our differences.

When we respectfully request a mediator, we are engaging in an attractive form of communication because we are communicating our desire to work "with each other" as opposed to "against each other." We are "agreeing to disagree" and maintaining a cooperative attitude, despite our differences. By agreeing to mediate, we are working to avoid lawsuits and unnecessary contention, giving ourselves many benefits compared with litigation. Nine attractive benefits of mediation are as follows:

First, mediation is a process that focuses on the future and not the past. With mediation, we do not keep "putting salt on our old wounds." Instead, we consider ways of working together to make the future better.

Second, mediation fosters creativity in the resolution of disputes. In litigation, there is typically a winner and a loser. In mediation, we instead concentrate on a cooperative win/win strategy wherein all parties can derive benefits. We are free to choose creative solutions that the legal system simply cannot or will not afford us.

Third, mediation enables us to control the process of communication and dispute resolution. In litigation, the process is largely dictated by legal rules and procedures. However, in mediation, we are free to work together and agree on the procedures that best serve our collective interests. We—not judges—choose the time, manner, and duration of the process of dispute resolution.

Fourth, mediation enables us to control the outcome of our disputes. In litigation, the outcome is determined by a judge or a jury. In mediation, we ourselves control our own outcome. We ourselves determine the terms of our agreement. In essence, we ourselves become the judge and the jury.

Fifth, mediation promotes confidentiality in the process and outcome of dispute resolution. The process and outcome of litigation are largely open to the public. Mediation is typically a confidential process, and the outcome can be made private by the terms of the agreement itself.

Sixth, mediation facilitates settlement compliance. In mediation, we ourselves choose the terms of our agreement. Therefore, we are typically more likely to comply rather than resist because we feel comfortable with the terms of the agreement we helped create. In litigation, the judgment is imposed upon us. Most of us do not like to be controlled or have judgments forced upon us. That is one of the reasons why many cases get appealed.

Seventh, mediation significantly reduces legal fees and costs. Legal fees and costs are often unpredictable and often can even exceed the amount in dispute. At the end of the litigation process, even in victory, our finances could be "in the red." In mediation, we typically pay for a set number of hours with a mediator at a set rate. The mediator's fees very often tend to be a small fraction of the total fees and costs incurred in litigation.

Eighth, mediation significantly reduces opportunity costs and stress. Opportunity costs are costs we incur because we lose the time or opportunity to do something else. Litigation can deprive us of many years of our time, effort, peace of mind, and opportunity. Even if some money is left over once our legal fees and costs are paid, after adjusting for our opportunity costs and stress, we could very well again be "in the red." In mediation, the resolution happens quickly—often in one session or one day!

Ninth, mediation allows us to maintain our personal or business relationships. In litigation, because we are adversaries fighting each other, we can severely damage our personal and business relationships—we are "working against each other." In mediation, we are simply trying to communicate and resolve our differences amicably; we are "working with each other."

ACTION PLAN FOR MEDIATION

WAY 255 If you are at an impasse in a personal or business dispute, consider the many benefits of mediation.

Once you make the choice to mediate, commit to the mediation process and **WAY 256** proceed with good faith.

WAY 257 Communicate your desire to mediate to the other party, highlighting the fact that you would like to work together as a team.

Communicate the many benefits of mediation to the other party. **WAY 258**

WAY 259 Work with the other party to jointly select a mediator you are both comfortable with.

Make sure that you select a mediator who is highly skilled in communication **WAY 260** because communication is the foundation of mediation.

There are interesting variations of classical mediation that may be attractive in difficult impasse situations. The mediation variations include *mediator-selection mediation, med-arb, high-low med-arb,* and *arb-med.* The purpose of these variations is to set forth a structure in which, no matter what, the dispute will indeed be resolved at the end of the varied mediation session. These variations all offer resolution and finality, even in the most difficult situations.

In what I refer to as *mediator-selection mediation,* the parties involved in a dispute first mediate their dispute but agree that, on impasse, the mediator has the power to select either the position of one party, or the position of the other party, but nothing in between. In other words, if the mediation is not successful, each party would write down his or her final best offer and hand it to the mediator. The mediator then decides which offer is the most reasonable. The most reasonable offer then becomes the ultimate binding outcome or result.

This process encourages each party to be as reasonable as possible because only the most reasonable offer is accepted by the mediator. Parties who get greedy risk having their offer rejected in its entirety.

In *med-arb*, the parties start off with classical mediation. However, the parties agree in advance that if there is an impasse after mediation, the mediator will become the arbitrator or final decision maker. At the end of the mediation, if there is no agreement, the mediator wears the hat of an arbitrator and makes a binding decision after hearing the evidence from all the parties to the dispute.

High-low med-arb is a modified form of *med-arb*. The parties involved in a dispute first mediate their dispute but agree that if there is an impasse, the mediator becomes the arbitrator and has the power to resolve their dispute. However, unlike a typical arbitration wherein an arbitrator has the freedom to decide an outcome without any pre-established parameters, in a *high-low process*, the parties jointly reduce their exposure level by determining a *high* (a ceiling or high point) and a *low* (a floor or low point). The decision or award of the arbitrator must fall somewhere between the *high* and the *low*. For example, in a mediation, if the best offer of one party to a dispute was to take a $100,000 to settle the dispute and the best offer of the other party was to pay $50,000 to settle the dispute, the parties can jointly agree on a *high* of $100,000 and a *low* of $50,000 as the parameters of a binding decision by the arbitrator. That way, the parties can have comfort in knowing that, no matter what, the ultimate resolution by the arbitrator on impasse will not be below $50,000. It also will not be more than $100,000.

Arb-med requires an arbitration to be conducted first. Evidence is heard, and the arbitrator makes a decision and writes down an award. The award is confidential, is sealed, and will not be communicated to any party to the dispute unless the parties cannot settle their dispute on their own. After the confidential award, the arbitrator puts on a "mediation hat" and mediates the dispute. If the parties themselves do not reach a settlement within their mediation session, the prior sealed award becomes the final award. This process encourages the parties to strive to reach a settlement on their own to avoid the unknown arbitrator award that will be imposed on them within seconds of a failed mediation.

ACTION PLAN FOR MEDIATION VARIATIONS

WAY 261
If you are communicating with a greedy or unreasonable person, offer to do a *mediator-selection mediation*. Because the mediator will simply throw out the most unreasonable offer, the more unreasonable the offer of the party opposing you will be, the more likely the mediator will adopt your position.

Consider a *med-arb* or *arb-med* if you want to first try to settle the matter

WAY 262

voluntarily but want a final binding outcome in the event your settlement discussions fail.

WAY 263
Consider a *high-low med-arb* if you seek a final resolution with limitations on what the arbitrator can award.

PART VI:

INTRAPERSONAL COMMUNICATION

ATTRACTIVE COMMUNICATION
CHAPTER 55
INNER GRATITUDE MESSAGING

What I refer to as *inner gratitude messaging* is the process of thanking the source of our existence for our many blessings and reminding ourselves of those blessings every day. Incorporating gratitude as a regular part of our self-talk is one of the most powerful things that we can do to instantly make our communications more attractive with ourselves and with others.

Gratitude creates an attractive, rewarding, happy energy. When we are thankful, we feel better from within. Moreover, when we appreciate the things that we have, we complain less and smile more. As a result, both our verbal communication (in terms of complaining less) and our non-verbal communication (in terms of smiling more) become more attractive.

ACTION PLAN FOR INNER GRATITUDE MESSAGING

Be thankful to the source of your existence and count your blessings every

WAY 264

day. Thanksgiving Day is a gratitude day that many treasure once a year. It is a day full of warmth, joy, and good energy. I invite you to celebrate a day of thanksgiving each and every day because you are, in fact, blessed each and every day. The more thankful you are and the more you count your blessings, the happier you will become. As you become happier with your life, you will complain less and smile more. Your communication will thus become powerfully more attractive.

WAY 265

Certain individuals complain that they will not be thankful to the source of their existence because they have not, as they put it, seen the source of their existence. I see the source of my existence through life's blessings every day. If you believe that you have not seen the source of your existence, imagine that you are sitting in a fine restaurant and have just enjoyed a delicious meal. However, you never actually met or saw the chef. Even though you never met or saw the chef, would you still be thankful to the chef for his or her preparation of your meal? I am confident that your answer would be yes. In fact, many people send their compliments to the chef they never met or saw. If you would be willing to thank the chef you never met or saw for a single meal, I invite you to thank the source of your existence for your entire life and the lives of the ones you love.

Some people complain that they do not know exactly how they were created, so

WAY 266

they refuse to thank the source of their existence for something they do not know the exact process of. If you are one of those individuals, consider your DNA. It entails intelligent, three-billion-lettered programming, information, and design. Consider your brain system, vision system, auditory system, taste system, sensation system, circulatory system, respiratory system, digestive system, endocrine system, skeletal system, reproductive system, and so on. These systems also entail intelligent programming, information, and design. Consider the incredibly precise life-sustaining systems of our planet earth. These systems also entail intelligent programming, information, and design. When there is a program, there is a programmer! When there is information, there is an informant! When there is a design, there is a designer!

We do not necessarily need to know the exact design of the things we have in order to appreciate them. In fact, most of us do not know the exact creative programming or design of many of the things we appreciate. For example, most of us do not know the exact programming of the computer software programs that we use. Most of us do not even know the exact creative designs of our televisions, telephones, radios, cars, etc. If you are thankful for the programming, information, and design that went into the creation of these products, I invite you to be thankful for the programming, information, and design that created and sustains your life and the lives of your loved ones.

WAY 267

Certain individuals complain that because bad things happen in life that they do not want to be thankful to the source of their existence. If you are one of those individuals, I ask that you imagine a world with no consequences, no incentives, no choices, no causes, no effects, and no free will—a world in which only "good" automatically happens, without the possibility of a "lesser good." If only good is supposed to happen "no matter what," then effort and choices would carry no real meaning or effect.

Even random accidents, unfavorable events, and unfavorable actions serve useful purposes. They teach us lessons and encourage us to think, grow, evolve, and seek solutions. Moreover, "goodness" is perceived only because of a comparative reference point of a "lesser good" or a "bad." In addition, when you know that at any time you can lose the things you have, you value them more. Indeed, life is real and precious because it was intelligently designed to entail consequences, incentives, causes, effects, free will, and lack of automatic perfection. I invite you to celebrate the reality and preciousness of your life.

Certain individuals believe they cannot # WAY 268

experience gratitude because they are

unlucky. If that applies to you, imagine that you entered a contest wherein you are supposed to pick the one winning number out of approximately one trillion other numbers. That seems near impossible to accomplish, right? Well, as it turns out, you have already won a contest with even tougher odds than that. A typical male produces approximately one trillion sperm in his lifetime. The fact is that you grew from the one winning sperm out of approximately a trillion that successfully fertilized one of the many eggs that made you the physical being that you are. Congratulations! You, indeed, were born lucky. I invite you to celebrate your luck.

WAY 269

Certain other individuals complain that they do not have enough valuable possessions. If that applies to you, I ask you whether you would trade your heart, brain, lungs, and eyes for two million dollars? If not, then you, in fact, are currently the owner of things that are more valuable than millions of dollars. I invite you to celebrate being rich.

ATTRACTIVE COMMUNICATION
CHAPTER 56
ATTRACTIVE IMAGINATION

Each and every day, we activate our brains to process images. Our imaginations largely serve as the languages of our brains because we often think in image patterns and pictures. What I refer to as *attractive imagination* is the process of communicating with our brains through imagination that is attractive. *Attractive imagination* encourages us, excites us, energizes us—and can make us happy. Unattractive imagination discourages us, promotes fear, makes us weaker—and can make us feel sad. Although we cannot immediately and fully control everything in life, we have significant control over our imaginations. Six important ways we can make our imaginations more attractive and effective follow.

First, we should positively imagine things, not as they relate to problems, fears, and worries, but as they relate to desires and solutions. If we visualize things that relate to problems, fears, or worries, we propel our conscious and subconscious mind to search our memory bank for thoughts, actions, and experiences that are consistent with those problems, fears, or worries. Then our focus and interactions in the future will also be based on such negativity. However, if we imagine desires and solutions, then they become the dominant directives for our brains. As a result, we will be directing both our conscious and subconscious mind to search our memory bank for every thought, action, plan, idea, or experience that aligns with desires and solutions. Imagining positive things assists our mind to do everything it can to provide us with the highest prospects, potential, and opportunities in the universe. Our minds work for us and not against us.

Second, whenever possible, we should imagine with all of our senses, such as sight, hearing, taste, smell, and touch. We should also feel the related emotion(s). For example, if we desire a new car, we should not only imagine the beautiful look of our new car, but also imagine hearing the engine roaring, smelling the distinctive "new car smell," and touching the steering wheel. We should also imagine feeling proud of ourselves for earning this new car. Using our five senses whenever possible—along with the feel of our emotion(s)—will reinforce the beneficial impact of our positive imaginations.

Third, we must imagine through our own eyes or in "first person" rather than "from the outside." This way, we elevate the magnitude of our experience because we are actually experiencing it. We're not watching a movie with us in it. Because we live in "first person," we should imagine in "first person."

Fourth, we must imagine repetitively. The more we imagine our desires, the stronger our neural pathways and brain connections associated with those desires become. Consequently, it will become easier for our conscious and subconscious mind to get what we want from the universe. By consistently and repetitively imagining what we want, we maximize our prospects, opportunities, and potential.

Fifth, we must imagine in detail, bringing in colors, shapes, sizes, and as much specificity as possible. The more specific we make our imaginations, the more impact we will have.

Sixth, we must treat our imaginations as though they are real and actually happening. In other words, we must experience the feeling of already having our desires in a real manner. The more real the experience of our imaginations, the more beneficial our imaginations will be.

ACTION PLAN FOR ATTRACTIVE IMAGINATION

At least once a day, imagine in a positive way the most important and productive **WAY 270** things that you want in life. Remember, this is your visualization; you have the power to imagine exactly what you want, the way you want it. So block out all negativity, problems, fears, and worries. Encourage your conscious and subconscious mind to gather every thought, action, plan, idea, or experience that could help you achieve whatever you want. Don't let your conscious and subconscious mind go negative and prevent you from getting what you want. Activate it to work for you, not against you.

WAY 271
Incorporate sight, hearing, taste, smell, touch, emotion, and lots of detail in your imaginations.

Imagine you are, in a real manner, experiencing in "first person" whatever you desire.
WAY 272

ATTRACTIVE COMMUNICATION
CHAPTER 57
INNER DECLARATIONS

Every day, we make declarations and communicate those declarations to ourselves through our self-talk. These declarations can either be attractive or unattractive. *Attractive declarations* bring us closer to our goals and desires. *Unattractive declarations* move us away from them.

Once we formally declare that we will, in fact, reach our goals, we become more attracted to success, and success becomes more attracted to us. Our attraction to success results from our belief in ourselves. Success's attraction to us happens because of our declaration to the universe that we are ready, willing, and able to earn and accept success. If we say we will, we will maximize our "will." If we say we won't, we will maximize our "won't."

ACTION PLAN FOR INNER DECLARATIONS

WAY 273
Make a list of all of your productive goals. Make them realistic but also aim high. Declare that you will achieve these goals. For each goal you declare that you want to achieve, declare anything and everything about you that might help you in reaching that goal. If you currently do not possess the skills or opportunities to achieve your goals, declare that you are ready, willing, and able to acquire the skills and opportunities you want.

If your goal is to find love, confidently declare that you will have the love you # WAY 274
seek. You could also make the following positive declarations:

"I seek love because I am a loving person."

"I'm open to love, and my openness maximizes my chances for experiencing love."

"I have the ability and willingness to learn everything I possibly can about love, thus maximizing my chances of experiencing love."

"When I have opened my heart in the past, there was a time when love has radiated through me and/or others."

"I love myself; therefore, I am capable of love."

"I have the ability to express myself in a loving way. Because love attracts love, I will attract love."

"Love is a part of a human's life, and because I am a human, love is a part of me."

WAY 275

If your goal is to become healthier, declare that you will be as healthy as possible. You could also make the following positive declarations:

"I now choose to fully inform myself about the health issues affecting me. Because I will gather the best information, I will maximize my health."

"I love myself and will take good care of myself."

"Because I care, I will maximize my health."

"I'm mentally strong and will easily recover from anything that comes my way."

"I'm physically strong and will easily recover from whatever comes my way."

"I'm emotionally strong and will easily recover from whatever comes my way."

"I'm spiritually strong and will easily recover from anything that comes my way."

If you have a goal of becoming wealthy, declare that you will be wealthy. You could also make the following positive declarations:

WAY 276

"I'm willing to work for my wealth, and because I'm not lazy, my chances of success are maximized."

"I'm dedicated to having the best communication skills, and because businesses are run by people, my ability to communicate effectively with people will maximize my wealth."

"I keep myself informed. Because knowledge creates opportunities, my knowledge will create wealth for me."

"I will work hard to attain a graduate degree which will eventually create opportunities for me."

"I have a lot of common sense that will help me deal with any roadblocks to attaining wealth."

"I'm a creative person, and I know that my creativity will help me find a niche that will make me wealthy."

ATTRACTIVE COMMUNICATION
CHAPTER 58
INNER OPTIMISM MESSAGING

People are attracted to people who believe in them and appreciate them. Words that are elevating, encouraging, and appreciative attract and motivate others—they are words that turn people on.

Words that are debasing, discouraging, and unfairly critical make people run the other way—they are words that turn people off. The same dynamic applies to us. Through our "self-talk" communication, we can turn ourselves "on" and "off."

Because people who think optimistically believe that goals can be reached, they typically communicate with themselves in the language of *optimism messaging*. This kind of messaging brings about encouragement that, in turn, facilitates accomplishment. Clearly, we cannot hear the music if our radios are turned off. *Optimism messaging* turns *on* our radios so we can pick up the radio signals in the universe and hear the music.

ACTION PLAN FOR INNER OPTIMISM
MESSAGING

WAY 277 Look at the glass as half full and not as half empty.

Have hope. Without it, your conscious and subconscious mind stops scanning # WAY 278 the universe for ways to make your dreams come true.

WAY 279 Ask yourself if there is anything in the past you accomplished that pleasantly surprised you. If yes, then remind yourself it can happen again. You could say something like this:

"I achieved_____ when I _____. I can make it happen again."

"I attracted the right people into my life when I _____. I will repeat these actions now."

"I was successful at_____ when I _____. I can do it again."

ATTRACTIVE COMMUNICATION
CHAPTER 59
INNER RESILIENCE MESSAGING

When something goes wrong, we tend to communicate with ourselves through self-talk. Our self-talk affects our response in very significant ways. If we attractively communicate to ourselves that "we will get through it" or "the problem will get resolved" or "we are strong" or "we can manage" or "we have been through worse and came out fine," then we give ourselves the gift of *resilience messaging*.

Resilience messaging allows us to be alert, proactive, productive, and creative. It allows us to look forward rather than backward, to be progressive rather than regressive, and to focus on solutions rather than problems. *Resilience messaging* sends a signal that we are strong—a strength signal.

Conversely, if we use self-talk consisting of fault, blame, resentment, or exaggeration, we create *negative messaging*. This kind of messaging negatively affects our response. Moreover, it signals to others that we are weak.

Most of the time, our best efforts are indeed good enough for resolving our problems. However, what if we don't achieve the desired solution as expected, despite our best efforts? Again, the concept of inner resilience messaging applies. Instead of using words of self-pity or anger, we could say something like this:

"This was a great learning experience."

"You can't get an education like this anywhere."

"Having gone through this, I can now get through anything."

Indeed, the benefits of a lesson learned might well exceed the costs of the initial problem.

ACTION PLAN FOR INNER RESILIENCE MESSAGING

Identify the names of the parties you believe contributed to or caused the # WAY 280

problem you are facing. When communicating with yourself, don't use those names. Instead, replace them with the names of people who can help you resolve your problem.

WAY 281 When communicating with yourself, identify all words that pertain to the history of the problem you are facing. Then replace those words with ones that pertain to the future.

When communicating with yourself, identify all words that pertain to the **WAY 282** causes of the problem you are facing. Replace those words with ones that pertain to solutions.

WAY 283 When communicating with yourself, identify all words that refer to the hardships you believe your problem has caused you. Replace those words with ones that pertain to valuable lessons you have learned.

ATTRACTIVE COMMUNICATION
CHAPTER 60
INNER FEAR MESSAGING

Messages of fear that are part of our daily self-talk can be either helpful or harmful. The key to attractive inner communication, as it pertains to fear, is to be selective with what we fear. It is important to choose between fears that *help* and fears that *hurt*. Helpful fears include the fear of touching something that could burn our skin, the fear of drinking alcohol and driving, the fear of smoking, the fear of unprotected intimate relations, the fear of speeding excessively, and so on.

There are also hurtful fears. In the area of communication, one is the fear of public speaking. This fear must be excluded from our self-talk because it can keep us from expressing our thoughts to larger social and business audiences. To justify our avoidance of public speaking, we might argue that we don't want to sound stupid or be embarrassed.

However, if we diligently prepare our thoughts and communicate them effectively and respectfully, people will be persuaded or at least will be respectful. If they act rudely and disrespectfully when we speak, that is their concern, not ours. Still, we can benefit because we obtain information about such people.

Fear of approaching others in social or business settings is another hurtful fear to be avoided. To justify our avoidance of approaching and engaging others to communicate, we might argue that "if we do not approach _____, we won't have to deal with the pain of rejection." However, in this case, *rejection* is not being avoided; *information* is being avoided.

In the world, billions of introductions have been made that led to successful personal or business relationships. Not everyone is a right match for us. Also, we are not a right match for everyone.

If we're not a match for someone or if someone is not a match for us, learning that truth is *information*, not *rejection*. We can guarantee getting valuable information if we approach others and if we communicate with them. However, if we never take those steps, we guarantee not knowing what could have been.

Action Plan for Inner Fear Messaging

When you speak in public, as long as you are prepared and communicate attractive- **WAY 284** ly, you will be respected. People may not always agree with you, but they will respect you. If they don't, it is their problem, not yours.

WAY 285

Feel free to approach others and communicate in social and business settings. Realize that any response you get in return is *information*, not *rejection*. When communicating with yourself, say something like this: "I believe in the value of information, so I'm going to get the valuable information no matter what the response will be."

When communicating with yourself, also say something like this: # WAY 286

"I'm proud of myself for making an effort and guaranteeing I receive valuable information."

ATTRACTIVE COMMUNICATION
CHAPTER 61
INNER KEYS

M any of us do not hold the keys to our happiness. Many of us have significantly, if not entirely, turned over the keys to our happiness to other people and external circumstances. When we tell ourselves that our happiness depends entirely on outside factors, we are communicating unattractive messages of weakness and uncertainty. We are left weak because we cannot always control our external environment and everyone around us. We are also left feeling uncertain because we cannot always know how other people will behave and what events will transpire.

Conversely, if we communicate to ourselves that we ourselves hold the keys to our happiness, we convey highly attractive messages of inner power and predictability. We have the power to control how we feel because we do not depend on others and external events to make us happy. We feel more certain because we know what we need to do for ourselves, by ourselves, to make us happy. Because we know ourselves, we know more and wonder less.

Once we communicate to ourselves that happiness comes from within, are we then isolating ourselves? No. Instead, we are choosing what works in our lives and leaving behind what doesn't work. We have better social and business interactions because we no longer depend on people who continually disappoint us. We take the keys to our happiness away from those who bring us down, and then we send them on their way. In their place, we surround ourselves with people who elevate us.

ACTION PLAN FOR INNER KEYS

WAY 287 Tell yourself that although you cannot always control other people and events, you yourself can control how you react to those people and events.

Tell yourself that you control what happens within you. # WAY 288

WAY 289 Take back the keys to your happiness from those who bring you down. Make a list of all people in your life who are hurting you. If, despite your best efforts, you conclude they are not a match for you, stop interacting with them. If it is not possible to entirely keep them out of your life, at least keep them from affecting your happiness. Remember, if you take away their keys to the doors to your happiness, then they can't come in.

Make a list of things that make you # WAY 290
unhappy. If you can make changes, do
so. If certain circumstances are not within your control, do not empower those circumstances to take away your happiness. Re-label "bad events" as "learning events." Communicate to yourself that these "learning events" will make you happier in the long run.

WAY 291
Make a list of all the things you have achieved in your life. Remind yourself that you had the power, means, and ability to bring about those achievements. You did it before and you can do it again! You are amazing! People cannot hurt you or get in your way if you do not let them!

ATTRACTIVE COMMUNICATION
CHAPTER 62
INNER STRESS REDUCTION

Stress and communication are indeed related. Stress affects how we feel, act, and talk. It affects the look in our eyes, the tone of our voice, our gestures, our energy level, and more. Stress can drain us and be highly visible to others. Clearly, as we reduce our stress levels, we elevate the attractiveness of our verbal and non-verbal communications.

ACTION PLAN FOR INNER STRESS REDUCTION

Count your blessings every day. **WAY 292**

WAY 293 Take good care of your physical body. Get an appropriate amount of sleep and safely engage in responsible physical activities that you like.

Do not use drugs. Do not drink exces- **WAY 294** sively. Drug use and heavy drinking are highly unattractive. If you use drugs or get drunk, your communication and public image will crash.

WAY 295 Use self-talk stress relievers to lower your stress. Reduce your level of complaints, communicate messages of hope and reassurance to yourself, and re-label problems as learning experiences. Focus on your goals and the related beneficial qualities and traits you already do possess. Take control of what happens *within* you (irrespective of what happens *to* you). Don't worry about things you cannot control, and limit the frequency of times you rush to judgment about people or events in life.

Take time-outs from any stress you feel. **WAY 296** Consider meditating one to three times a day. Meditation can shift your attention away from stressful issues to something that relaxes you—or to nothing at all.

WAY 297 Do deep breathing several times a day. Deep breathing can shift your focus away from the issues giving you stress to breathing in the oxygen that sustains the miracle of your life.

Watch funny movies or videos that make you laugh.

WAY 298

WAY 299

Consider listening to relaxing music or engaging in a hobby of your choice that is relaxing in nature.

Visualize the things that make you happy. Visualization can shift your atten-

WAY 300

tion away from stressful issues to images that are beautiful and appealing to you. In effect, visualization can provide you with your own beautiful sanctuary.

Attractive Communication
Conclusion

You have now read these 300 ways to make your communications more attractive. Have you thought about how you will apply them to your communications and circumstances? I invite you to immediately start using as many as you can when communicating with friends, family, loved ones, co-workers, business partners, business associates—and everyone else in your life.

As you put them into action, you will see every part of your life become increasingly more attractive. This is because communication substantially and substantively affects each and every part of your life every day.

ATTRACTIVE COMMUNICATION
ABOUT THE AUTHOR

After receiving his business degree in 1990, Michael Rooni went to law school for formal education and training in law and mediation. In 1992, he started mediating and helping people resolve their disputes in a cooperative and peaceful manner. He earned his doctorate in jurisprudence in 1993 and has been a member of the State Bar of California since 1994. He is an appointee to the Los Angeles Superior Court Voluntary Settlement Conference Panel.

Mr. Rooni has helped resolve very complex and contentious personal, business, and legal conflicts through litigation, mediation, and communication consulting. Currently, he mediates high-conflict disputes and trains corporate employees, business owners, couples, and individuals in the fields of communication and dispute resolution. He has participated in, observed, and studied thousands of communications in his search for the most attractive and effective communication and dispute resolution methods.

Mr. Rooni is a sought-after, high-impact speaker, practitioner, and consultant in the fields of communication and dispute resolution.